ATTITUDES
OF GREAT LEADERS

Bringing Down the Giants
In Your Life

ATTITUDES
OF GREAT LEADERS

BRINGING DOWN THE GIANTS
IN YOUR LIFE

by
BISHOP RICK FARLEY

Destiny Image® Publishers, Inc.
P.O. Box 310
Shippensburg, PA 17257-0310

*"Speaking to the Purposes of God for this Generation
and for the Generations to Come."*

For Worldwide Distribution, Printed in the U.S.A.

ISBN 10: 0-7684-2359-7
ISBN 13: 978-0-7684-2359-4

This book and all other Destiny Image, Revival Press, MercyPlace, Fresh Bread, Destiny Image Fiction, and Treasure House books are available at Christian bookstores and distributors worldwide.

For a U.S. bookstore nearest you, call
1-800-722-6774.

For more information on foreign distributors, call
717-532-3040.

Or reach us on the Internet:
www.destinyimage.com

1 2 3 4 5 6 7 8 9 10 11 / 09 08 07 06

#150329084

DEDICATION

Dedicated lovingly to Karren, my wife, who has never failed me. She is my loving partner and companion who has always believed in me and stood beside me through the bad times and the good times for 35 years.

And to Steve Poland for his help with sentence structure and punctuation.

2 SAMUEL 23:8-39 (NKJV):

These are the names of the mighty men whom David had: Josheb-Basshebeth the Tachmonite, chief among the captains. He was called Adino the Eznite, because he had killed eight hundred men at one time. And after him was Eleazar the son of Dodo, the Ahohite, one of the three mighty men with David when they defied the Philistines who were gathered there for battle, and the men of Israel had retreated. He arose and attacked the Philistines until his hand was weary, and his hand struck to the sword. The Lord brought about a great victory that day; and the people returned after him only to plunder. And after him was Shammah the son of Agee the Hararite. The Philistines had gathered together into a troop where there was a piece of ground full of lentils. So the people fled from the Philistines. But he stationed himself in the middle of the field, defended it, and killed the Philistines. So the Lord brought about a great victory.

Then three of the thirty chief men went down at harvest time and came to David at the cave of Adullam. And the troop of Philistines encamped in the Valley of Rephaim.

David was then in the stronghold, and the garrison of the Philistines was then in Bethlehem. And David said with longing, 'Oh, that someone would give me a drink of the water from the well of Bethlehem, which is by the gate!' So the three mighty men broke through the camp of the Philistines, drew water from the well of Bethlehem that was by the gate, and took it and brought it to David. Nevertheless he would not drink it, but poured it out to the Lord. And he said, 'Far be it from me, O Lord, that I should do this! Is this not the blood of the men who went in jeopardy of their lives?' Therefore he would not drink it. These things were done by the three mighty men.

Now Abishai the brother of Joab, the son of Zeruiah, was chief of another three. He lifted up his spear against three hundred men, killed them, and won a name among these three. Was he not the most honored of three? Therefore he became their captain. However, he did not attain to the first three. Benaiah was the son of Jehoiada, the son of a valiant man from Kabzeel, who had done many deeds. He had killed two lion-like heroes of Moab. He also had gone down and killed a lion in the midst of a pit on a snowy day.

And he killed an Egyptian, a spectacular man. The Egyptian had a spear in his

hand; so he went down to him with a staff, wrested the spear out of the Egyptian's hand, and killed him with his own spear. These things Benaiah the son of Jehoiada did, and won a name among three mighty men. He was more honored than the thirty, but he did not attain to the first three. And David appointed him over his guard. Asahel the brother of Joab was one of the thirty; Elhanan the son of Dodo of Bethlehem.

Shammah the Harodite, Elika the Harodite, Helez the Paltite, Ira the son of Ikkesh the Tekoite. Abiezer the Anathothite, Mebunnai the Hushathite, Zalmon the Ahohite, Maharai the Netophathite, Heleb the son of Baanah (the Netophathite), Ittai the son of Ribai from Gibeah of the children of Benjamin, Benaiah a Pirathonite, Hiddai from the brooks of Gaash, Abi-Albon the Arbathite, Azmaveth the Barhumite, Eliahba the Shaalbonite (of the sons of Jashen), Jonathan, Shammah the Hararite, Ahiam the son of Sharar the Hararite, Eliphelet the son of Ahasbai, the son of the Maachathite, Eliam the son of Ahithophel the Gilonite, Hezrai the Carmelite, Paarai the Arbite, Igal the son of Nathan of Zobah, Bani the Gadite, Zeleck the Ammonite, Naharai the Beerothite (armorbearer of Joab the son of Zeruiah), Ira the Ithrite, Gareb the Ithrite, and Uriah, the Hittite; thirty-seven in all.

CONTENTS

INTRODUCTION

W HILE I have served in leadership positions over the past 34 years of ministry, I do not consider myself an authority on leadership. I have read many leadership books and articles over the years that were written by men whom I admire for their knowledge and expertise, and their writings have given me help in my own ministry. However, much of my life has consisted of trial-and-error lessons I've received through on-the-job training.

What I have longed for is biblical truth, not a business education. While the church is like a business in some respects, and a great deal of help has come through business-centered leadership principles, I have always felt that spiritual leaders need to practice leadership principles that are supplied by the Holy Spirit as they endeavor to find and give direction to the Lord's church and ministries.

The purpose of this book is to examine principles of leadership from a completely biblical perspective by showing how King David, one of the Bible's greatest leaders, was able to motivate men and pour his own attitudes and skills into his team.

This book takes a close look at the attitudes of leaders that lead to success. It shows how David's teams exercised proper leadership attitudes and actions that helped make David into Israel's greatest warrior leader.

Indeed, King David was a man who fulfilled the promises God that were made to Abraham and Moses through whom He built His kingdom by expanding its boundaries into the Promised Land.

I hope you will enjoy the stories, word studies, and interpretations I present in the following pages. The Bible has not said a great deal about the lives of these men, but it has recounted their exploits as leaders. Along the way, I have taken a few creative liberties through the use of my imagination as I've told their stories. I hope you will enjoy the results.

CHAPTER 1

KING DAVID'S
TEAM BUILDING

IMAGINE yourself climbing over a rise and looking down at a lush, green valley. There are neat rows of pea plants—symmetrical rows that have been plowed carefully by a farmer. The air is cool and moist on this particular early morning, but the sun is creeping over the far hills.

While you scan the fields below, you notice movement out of the corner of your eye. It's off to your right. You see a man standing in the field with his sword drawn, fighting through a crowd of warriors. Many are lying at his feet, dying. It appears that a whole troop of Philistines is trying to maneuver toward him.

As you work your way down the hill and get closer to the action, you begin to wonder why the man hasn't turned to run instead of staying there to fight against such seemingly impossible odds. You notice that his sword is swinging with such speed and ferocity that it's a blur. His clothing and arms are red with blood. As you draw closer, you begin to realize that you have seen this man before. All of a sudden it dawns on you that he is one of King David's men of valor, Shammah, the son of Agee!

In the following pages, I will share with you what I feel were the qualities that made King David's team into mighty men of valor—true leaders in their time. We will be talking about Adino, Eleazar, Shammah, Josheb-Basshebeth, Benaiah, Uriah, Eliam, and his father, Ahithophel.

These men caught the same vision David had for their lives and for all of Israel. They strengthened themselves together with him. They had little to offer to their king, but they did have a deep commitment to him. After all is said and done, it is not wealth that lasts after a man anyway; it is his reputation that continues to count. These men followed David because they knew he was a man of honor.

Integrity and Uprightness

David wrote this prayer: *"Let integrity and uprightness preserve me; for I wait for You"* (Ps. 25:21 NKJV). Another translation puts it this way, *"Let integrity and uprightness be my bodyguards."*

Both David and Solomon speak of integrity in the Psalms and Proverbs no less than 11 times. Solomon says, "He who walks in integrity walks securely."

Webster defines integrity as "an unimpaired condition, soundness, being complete or undivided, honesty, incorruptibility." The Hebrew word for "integrity" is translated as "soundness, simplicity, completeness or uprightness."

Integrity, therefore, is sincerity of heart and intention, truthfulness, uprightness, being sincere, honest, and pure of heart in all your intentions. What do you do when no one is watching? Can you say you do what is right all the time no matter what the cost might be? That is integrity!

Is integrity just a quaint relic of earlier times, a time when things were less complicated and people trusted a man's word as his bond? The integrity that David and Solomon valued so highly is as vital today as it was in ancient times. To build a team like David did, we need a commitment to integrity which sets us apart as children of God.

Many people today are cynical, skeptical, and suspicious of institutions, and many times that skepticism has been earned. Television programs such as "60 Minutes," "20/20," "Primetime," and others have made a franchise out of scandal.

A commitment to integrity reflects God's character to others. This is true because our God is a God of complete and perfect integrity! Numbers 23:19 (NIV) tells us that *"God is not man, that He should lie, nor a son of man, that he should change his mind. Does he speak and then not act? Does he promise and not fulfill?"* God always keeps His promises.

This is an essential truth, because the entire Christian religion is based on faith in God and His promises. If you don't walk in integrity you will never be secure, because you will always be worrying about covering your tracks, making sure your story is consistent, and making sure you didn't leave any clues that would eventually find you out.

Without integrity you will never build a team that will follow you. I still remember my father saying to me, "Son, your word is the greatest asset you have. Don't throw it away. If you tell a man you will be somewhere or do something for him and you shake hands on it, then be sure you keep that word, even if you have to walk over mountains and valleys to do it. Because your integrity and trust are at stake."

YOU CANNOT DO IT ALONE

Another key to David's effectiveness as a leader was that he didn't try to lead by himself. Regardless of your task, to be an effective leader (as a parent, a homemaker, a businessperson, an employee, or in any other capacity), *you must remember that you cannot do it alone.*

I once heard a minister say, "There isn't a single person in the world who can make a pencil." He continued this thought by examining what goes into the manufacturing of a pencil. He explained that the wood has to come from a tree that was cut by a lumberjack. The graphite has to be mined by miners in South America. The rubber for the eraser comes from a rubber tree on a Malaysian rubber plantation. It's true; it takes a countless number of people to make just one pencil.

To succeed as leaders, therefore, we need to recognize the necessity of having others of like mind working alongside us, sharing our vision and working toward a common goal.

CHOOSE THE WEAKEST ENEMY FIRST

In Second Samuel 8:1-3 we see that David was a warrior with a plan. David's strategy was to attack one enemy at a time. The first enemies he chose were those he had already defeated. Why did he choose the weakest enemy first? He did so because this would allow him to gain some victories for his team, and such victories would build the people's confidence. David always endeavored to instill confidence in his team by allowing them to be a part of his battles and by letting them share in his victories.

In our hometown, our high school always has a homecoming game to start off the football season. They have never lost their homecoming games. I once asked my son, "Why has your school never lost a homecoming game?"

He was quick to respond, "It's because they always schedule the homecoming games to be with schools they know they can beat."

No one wants to start off a sports season with a loss. The job of the coach is to build confidence and enthusiasm in his team for future wins.

David's strategy was much the same. He defeated the weakest enemies first, then he conquered those who were closest to Israel. Winning over those who are nearest to you is a necessity.

PUTTING THE INTERESTS OF OTHERS FIRST

Establishing military posts is a necessary strategy, as well. You need to monitor those you conquer and win to your side. I have seen pastors attacked and nearly destroyed by those they counted as their closest friends. In effect, David is saying, "Don't assume that those you have allowed to be near you will always be or stay on your side."

David continued to win the loyalty of those around him by putting their interests first.

"So David reigned over all Israel; and David administered judgment and justice to all his people" (2 Sam. 8:15 NKJV). He made sure the interests of the people were taken care of.

The reason why it is sometimes hard for leaders to put other people first may be insecurity, ego, or pride. Sometimes a leader is so goal-oriented that he or she just wants to get the job done. Some leaders feel they are placed in the positions they hold in order to be served instead of being a servant. But David was a man who empowered others to become what God had called them to be.

Each of David's men built a name for themselves while helping David achieve his own goals and fulfill the anointing on his life. I would say that David was not an insecure man. Rather, he was willing to let his leaders become what God had called them to be. This, in turn, added to his position and prestige. He was not afraid to delegate responsibilities to others.

David faced the challenge of conquering Jerusalem. He looked for ways to take the city. Therefore, he challenged his men by making a promise: he told them that the man who would find a way to take the walls of the city would become the leader of his armies.

LEADING BY EXAMPLE

Delegation is just a theory before it is put into practice. You need to recognize the ability of others as you build your team. One leadership principle I have heard over and over again is: "Those who are closest to me determine the level of my success."

Why were the men on David's team so committed to him?

It was because David led by example. He was a fearless man. As a boy he had faced a bear and a lion, and, according to his own testimony, he killed both of them. Then, as a young man, he faced Goliath, a 9-foot-tall Philistine warrior, in front of all Israel's fighting men, and David won! He inspired men of courage. I believe he would have even inspired men without courage to stand and wage war. David was not afraid to involve himself alongside those he led.

In a very real sense David lived and led according to the following statement: "WE TEACH THEM WHAT WE KNOW, WE REPRODUCE WHAT WE ARE!"

CHAPTER 2

THE LESSON OF ZIKLAG

L ET'S imagine David and his men returning from the battlefield; they're on their way home to their loved ones. When they are about a mile from home, one of the men points toward the horizon, in the direction of some smoke rising into the air. Soon they all see it and begin to wonder what is causing it. They drive their horses faster, into a gallop, as fear grips at their hearts.

As they get closer to the town of Ziklag, they realize that flames and smoke are rising from their homes and stables. They don't see anyone there, and no one runs out to meet them. No one is trying to put out the fires. When they arrive, their worst fears are realized. Everything they own and all that they love are missing, and their homes have been burned.

How do they respond to such a crisis?

In First Samuel 27 David asks Achish, the King of Gath, to give him a town that would be for him and his men. At this time David was on the run from King Saul and had decided to live in the land of the Philistines, hoping that this would stop Saul from chasing him. In response to his request, the King of Gath gave David the town of Ziklag.

Later, the king asked David and his men to go to war with him against Israel. The other Philistine kings were afraid of David. They went to Achish and asked him to send David and his men away. They were afraid that David would turn on them in the midst of battle and fight for the Israelites. David and his men left and returned home only to find their homes burned and their families kidnapped!

BOTH A DANGER AND AN OPPORTUNITY

It's interesting to take note of the Chinese word-symbol for a crisis. They use a combination of the symbols for both danger and opportunity to depict a crisis.

Everyone experiences crises in their lives. Some people become stronger as a result of these experiences, while others become weaker. A crisis can truly be an opportunity to learn and grow, and this was the approach David took toward crises that he and his team experienced.

The important thing is not what happens to us, but how we deal with what happens to us! There are both constructive and non-constructive ways of responding to any crisis. For one thing, we can deny that a problem exists and hide our head in the sand. Or we can attempt to evade the problem by turning to alcohol and drugs.

Another approach would be to refuse to seek help and try to handle it ourselves. We may even fail to seek God's help at times, waiting until we have tried every possible human angle before turning to Him.

Sometimes we may even be tempted to engage in "the blame-shift game," blaming others for our problems. For example, people may blame the crisis on society, DNA, or their upbringing. We may also fail to explore possible solutions because we figure they won't work anyway.

Through David's example we see that the right way is to face the problem, even if it is not your fault, to separate what is changeable from the unchangeable, and to seek help when we are exploring ways to deal with a problem or a crisis.

As we do so, we need to remember the promises of God, such as this one: *"No temptation has seized you except what is common to man. And God is faithful: he will not let you be tempted beyond what you can bear. But when you are tempted, he will also provide a way out so that you can stand up under it"* (1 Cor. 10:13 NIV). In effect, this Scripture is saying: *"No crisis is more than what you can deal with through the help of God."*

We find another important promise of God in Romans 8:28: *"No situation is so bad but what some good can come from it"* (author's paraphrase).

Many times our first reaction when something tragic happens to us is to say that it is unfair. The tragic event might take the form of many different problems such as the loss of a loved one, the loss of property, the loss of a job, the loss of friends, an automobile wreck, a dry well, being laid off, a paycheck that bounces, no paycheck at all, or your kid turning to drugs. You try to do what is right in the midst of the crisis, but, instead, you find yourself being filled with feelings of disappointment and fighting feelings of despair!

David and his great men of war, even though they were strong, battle-hardened warriors, wept in bitter disappointment as they surveyed what had happened in their town of Ziklag and wondered what had become of their loved ones. In fact, the Bible says that *"they wept until they had no strength left to weep."*

When the devil takes your strength and resolve, you are no longer a threat to him! Disappointment and grief are often followed by people trying to find someone or something to blame.

Instead of pulling together in their time of need, David's friends and loyal companions began to find fault in him. The Bible says, *"Each one was bitter in their spirits because of his sons and daughters."*

Maybe they figured that David should have left a bigger guard behind to protect the village or should have had some kind of contingency plan in place. Perhaps they blamed David because he took them to a war that they felt wasn't theirs. Whatever theirs motives, in their hearts they wanted to destroy him.

A CRISIS IN LEADERSHIP

One thing is certain: this was a crisis in leadership! Unresolved bitterness is a weapon the enemy often uses against a team, because he knows that wounded people wound others! No one is immune to pain, hurt, or suffering. If feelings of bitterness are not dealt with, they will always resurface somewhere later.

David cried until he couldn't cry anymore. His sorrow and his fears were just as real as those of his men. David was distressed and his men started picking up stones to hurl at him. As a godly leader of his men, he was at his wit's end, but he was not at faith's end. Believers have a right to trust their God when times are the worst. God says that He will be with us always. He also says that all things will work together for our good. (See Romans 8:28.)

There are certain godly principles to note here. First, we must rise up. Second, we must pursue, and, third, we must recover all. Don't lie down and give up, don't run, and don't stick your head in the sand. Face your problems with God's help! He is a very present help in your time of need. You can throw stones, or you can recover what the enemy has stolen from your spirit and life.

I've been told that more than 1,500 ministers leave their ministries every week in America. That statistic is tangible proof of the crises that leaders face in our present time. Leaders may run, hide, and try to pretend, hoping that their problems will go away, but we must remember that no one said leadership was going to be easy. There is no easy way to be a leader and no easy way to get through a crisis.

It is clear that David understood this truth as we see in this story about Ziklag. He was at a critical place in his life, and his very life was in danger. Today it may be your ministry that's in danger. Perhaps your team is turning against you because they are blaming a current situation on your leadership. What do you do in such a case?

You need to decide to rise up and pursue a solution. Take control of the situation by using your faith in God.

ENCOURAGE YOURSELF IN GOD

David's past experiences with the lion, the bear, the giant, and all the battles he had fought increased his trust in the God who had continually delivered him. David rose up and encouraged himself in God. The word "encourage" means "to make firm, to preserve, to be firm, to be strong, to bind fast, and to strengthen."

Yes, David had a problem. Did he have heartache, also? Yes, he clearly did. But did he have time to feel sorry for himself? No. David went to God for strength and firmness. In the process, something happened to David's attitude. He picked himself up, and his men noticed the change in him!

I would like to know what David prayed or what he meditated on, because whatever it was brought about an awesome change in his outlook, attitude, and behavior. Perhaps he had channeled his hurt and anguish into anger at the enemy instead of turning it in upon himself. He may have looked within and spoke to himself like he did in Psalm 42:11 (NKJV): *"Why are you cast down, O my soul? And why are you disquieted within me? Hope in God; For I shall yet praise Him. The help of my countenance and my God."*

YOUR ATTITUDE IS A CHOICE

A good team leader knows that his attitude is a choice! When you are in a crisis, do you let the devil keep you down? Do you let your emotions keep you down with feelings of hurt, bitterness, and confusion, or do you let God pick you up? Remember, your response and your attitude are choices you make.

Rise above the situation and make up your mind to pursue the enemy. In so doing you will get back your joy and peace! You will get back your blessing, as well! (I don't know how long it took in David's case, but the situation was highly explosive.) David shows us the difference between a leader who is a worshiper of God and one who isn't. The true worshiper's first inclination is to seek God! The true worshiper wants to know God's answer for the situation.

I believe that part of David's encouragement was found in the fact that he already knew his destiny. He could remember the day when Samuel the prophet had come to his father's house and poured a horn of oil over his head, anointing him to be the next king of Israel.

KEEP YOUR EYES ON YOUR DESTINY

Destiny is a predetermined victory that is delivered into your hands by God!

David had his eyes fixed on the destiny that God had promised to him. Have you ever seen those videos of people running their vehicles off the road into parked cars or police sedans? The reason why this happens is that the drivers are looking at another vehicle or a nearby accident and then they automatically drive in the direction toward which their eyes are fixed. Be sure to fix your eyes on your destiny in God and then follow the direction of your gaze!

Many of the things that happen in our lives and ministries are like alarm clocks in that they serve to move us out of our comfort zones and get us back on track with our planned destinies. They wake us up to the real issues of our lives.

Think about it, God's destiny for Israel was the land of Canaan. If they hadn't had to face persecution, they would never have pursued their destiny. They had been given the best land of all in Egypt with no taxation, and they had enjoyed the favor of Pharaoh in the days of Joseph. Who would have wanted to leave a place like that in order to find their destiny?

David shows us that when you know your destiny, you can get knocked down, but you will get back up! The Bible says the righteous can fall seven times, but they always get back up.

What makes them righteous? Part of it is found in the fact that they get back up and try again! David suffered a blow, but he knew what his destiny was in God. Therefore, he encouraged himself in God and chose to lead instead of feeling sorry for himself.

Moses was that kind of leader, as well. When he faced a crisis he would handle it by saying, "We'll let God decide." One day, Korah, one of Israel's leaders, rose up with 250 elders of the congregation.

Korah was a Levite, one of the company of men who were responsible for the house of God. However, he wanted Moses' job. He challenged Moses by saying in effect, "Who made you the boss? After all, we are all a part of the same body. What makes you something special?"

Moses didn't try to argue his way out of the situation. Nor did he try to negotiate with Korah. He didn't give him a list of his accomplishments for Korah to compare with his own. Rather, Moses fell on his face before God and then told Korah, "Let's let God make the choice."

In a similar vein, David's choice was God, and he asked the Lord if he should pursue his enemies.

God's answer was simple and direct: "Yes!"

When the enemy moves in and steals from you, you need to go after him and take back what is rightfully yours. This might be your joy, your peace, your love, your family, your children, or your salvation.

EVERY CRISIS IS A TIME FOR WARFARE

Every crisis is a time for warfare! It is not a time to give up and hope for the best. Don't ever accept what the enemy has for you. Doing so makes you his slave!

I remember one major family crisis the enemy sent our way. It was incredibly discouraging, fearful, and depressing. He hit every child in our family all at once. My oldest daughter, Felicia, learned that she had cancer. My next daughter, Christy, began to have fainting spells that left the doctors puzzled. My oldest son, Jason, broke his hip in basic training, and it looked as if the bone was dying and would have to be removed. In addition, my youngest son, Nathan, ran away from home. He was diagnosed as suffering from bi-polar disorder. Then he turned to crime, took numerous drugs, and even invited demon possession into his life.

As these horrendous things began to happen to my children, I immediately went to prayer and became very angry at the enemy. I said, "Devil, you cannot have my children! I refuse to give them up to you! They were all dedicated to God as babies, and I expect God's help to come forth now on their behalf."

Then I prayed for each child and placed them into God's capable hands. When I finished praying, I left encouraged, knowing in my heart that God had heard my prayer. I knew I had to go on in Him, and I told my wife, "Everything is going to be OK."

Before long, things began to happen! The doctors couldn't find any trace of cancer in my daughter. My other daughter has never had another fainting spell. We spoke life into the bone in my son's leg and it mended. The situation with our youngest son was the toughest, for it took a couple of years of turmoil and prayer to overcome it. Then, one day God spoke to me and said, *"If you will fast, I will deliver your son."* I fasted, and God saved him within a month. I'm happy to report that he is now in Bible school, and he's preaching and living for the Father.

Likewise, we faced a major church crisis, and with God's capable help, it is now moving forward, blessed by His Spirit and the spiritual health He provides for His children.

So, leader, rise above your situation and make up your mind to pursue the enemy.

I don't think it took David long to do this even though his situation was explosive, and men were searching the ground for stones to throw at him. Change and encouragement came as he sought God.

Get on the enemy's trail quickly while it is still hot. Start with prayer and follow the directions of the Lord. Don't waste time with anger or looking for someone else to blame. Fight the situation with all your might.

David didn't know which way to go or how big his foe was. He didn't know if their families were dead or alive, or if his army could make it. *But God did!*

The Bible tells us to stand fast in the liberty wherewith Christ has made us free, and be not entangled again in the yoke of bondage. (See Galatians 5:1.)

The word translated as "bondage" in this verse is from the Greek word, "douleia," which means: "servitude, a state of a man in which he is prevented from freely possessing and enjoying life."

Don't slip out of your liberty and be prevented by the enemy from possessing and enjoying life! Encourage yourself in the Lord! Strength comes by prayer and meditating on His truthful Word. Get up by faith, and chase down your enemy. This works with any enemy, including poverty, depression, anger, impatience, fear, worry, hurt, etc.

David's men saw a new David, one who said, "Let's go get our families back and kick some butt!" They no longer saw a depressed, weakened David. Instead, they saw a confident warrior.

What did David's new attitude cause? It caused the men to rise up and follow him, and eventually they were able to recover everything. In verses 18-19, they got it all back, plus some extra to share with others, and this enabled them to build some good will among the people.

The attitude that came out of the crisis of Ziklag was: I am an overcomer! The Bible says so, and I will not allow any situation to be bigger than my faith in God's ability.

UNDERSTAND GOD'S GREATER PURPOSE

Another method of dealing with conflict and tragedy such as what these men faced at Ziklag is to understand that a greater purpose is involved, and knowing that God has a purpose always helps you to put your trust and faith in God.

There is a story of another great man who understood God's grace in the midst of conflict and tragedy. I love this story; it is about a man named Job. It always intrigued me that Job named his daughters, not his sons, in Job 42:13-14 (NKJV): *"He also had seven sons and three daughters. And he called the name of the first Jemimah, the name of the second Keziah, and the name of the third Keren-Happuch."*

Usually in the Bible the names of sons are written, but it is very rare to find the names of daughters listed.

The story of Job concerns a test of Job's love for God. Satan had come before God in the first chapter of the Book of Job and said, *"Of course Job loves you; look at what you have done for him. He loves you for the things you can give him and do for him. He doesn't love you just for yourself."*

Many who have based their love for God on the blessings He can give instead of the sacrifice of Christ for their souls have fallen and many others will fall, as well, when things go wrong.

First, satan took Job's livelihood, including his oxen, sheep, and cattle, and then he even took his servants. Then he took his children, even though Job prayed and sacrificed to God daily for them. Still, Job loved God! His faith wasn't based on his prosperity, but on the God who had given the blessings.

Through all of his testing Job maintained his love for God. Finally, after all was said and done, Job shared what he had learned from his experience. This is why he gave us the names of his three daughters instead of the names of his sons. He recorded his experience in the names of his daughters, as we will see in the following paragraphs.

God has a goal! That goal is to break your outer shell and make you into more of a spiritual being. He is constantly working to mold you and make you into what He has destined for you to become in Him.

JEMIMAH—THE DOVE

Job's first daughter was named Jemimah. Her name in Hebrew means "the dove." This leads us to understand that the divine agent who has been sent by God to change our lives is the Holy Spirit, the dove of God.

I could preach forever and no one would change. I can challenge sin, but it's not my job to make you change. Change comes by the anointed Word and the Holy Spirit. God's job is change! It's the "heavenly dove," the convicting power of the Holy Spirit, that brings change into our hearts and lives. By giving the name of Jemimah to his daughter Job is telling us that the Spirit came to bring change in his life. He is declaring that all he went through was meant by God for his good and for the fulfillment of his destiny.

KEZIAH—A SEPARATION OF THE BARK

The second daughter's name was Keziah. Her name means "a separation of the bark." Names like this have to be of divine origin. I don't know any father who would call his daughter "the stripping off of the bark."

What is Job telling us through the name of his second daughter? I believe he is saying that the outer shell must be stripped from us by the Holy Spirit. God had enabled him to see that he was not all that he thought he was. In each of our lives God wants to break the outer shell so the light of His Spirit can shine through and be seen by others.

It's the Holy Spirit that bangs against our heads, attitudes, and hearts in order to bring about brokenness and humility. He skins the outer shells of hypocrisy, pride, and self-righteousness from our lives. If you strip the bark from a tree, it will die. God wants our outer man crucified to the cross so our inner man can live.

We see this happening in the life of Jacob, as well. Jacob took his brother's birthright and blessing. He tricked his uncle out of the best sheep. He sent his family and servants to face disaster. He was a proud and arrogant deceiver who ended up being stripped and changed by God. He ended his days leaning on his staff and prophesying his children's destinies in God and life.

God sends the Holy Spirit to get the bark off and smooth out the rough edges. His methods may come in the form of conflicts and tragedies, such as those experienced by David and his men at Ziklag.

Keren-Happuch—The Horn of Cosmetics

The last daughter was named Keren-Happuch. Her name means: "the horn of cosmetics" and it may be literally translated as "the horn of eye shadow." What are cosmetics and eye shadow? They are artificial beauty aids that cover one's natural appearance. Why do people use them? It's because they want to cover any natural blemishes that appear on their skin.

The use of the word "horn" in the Bible, as we see in both the Book of Daniel and in the Revelation of John, implies power or rule. So Job is saying that Keren-Happuch is the power of cosmetics. Remember, cosmetics are artificial aids that create a facade. They are used to cover what is real and natural.

God has come to remove all phoniness from our lives! He uses the Holy Spirit and times of personal conflict to remove our facades, the hypocrisy and the phoniness in our lives. He wants to remove the false fronts we put on for others to see.

God also wants to remove the blemishes we cover up. We may attempt to cover them with a smile or even with praise for the Lord. We do all of this even though we may be anxious, hurt, angry, bitter, and full of fears deep within. We attempt to cover these things with our "spiritual cosmetics."

Job says that God came to take the phony away. He is stripping off our outer shells to make us truly whole and natural before Him. How could Job still praise God on the ash heap while suffering with open sores all over his body? He had so many blemishes that no cosmetic could cover them!

Take a look in magazines at pictures of women before and after they go from plain to beautiful. Though the transformations are amazing, remember it's all external, for, only one thing can change the inside. It's only as we yield to God that we can expect those inner changes to come.

So let God apply His "spiritual cosmetics" to your life. Let Him perform whatever "cosmetic surgery" that may be needed.

What is cosmetic surgery? It involves God tearing off the outer shell so we will see the truth about our lives. It frequently takes place when we are on "the ash heap," scraping our wounds. Our "ash heap" may be tight finances, car wrecks, sickness, or others stresses and pressures.

It's at such times that you need to encourage yourself in God, standing firm in faith and saying, *"Though He slay me, yet will I trust Him"* (Job 13:15 NKJV).

CHAPTER 3

SHAMMAH, THE SON OF AGEE

(PERSEVERANCE)

WHEN we left Shammah (in the illustration opening Chapter 1), he was fighting for his life over a pea patch or a lentil patch, depending on which translation you use. As we watch Shammah, he slips to his knees in utter exhaustion. His arms are heavy and great drops of sweat fall from his brow. He is covered with blood and sweat, and some of the blood is his own. A few of the Philistine soldiers managed to get through his defenses, but these were just minor inconveniences to a man like Shammah.

Now let's continue with our imaginative look at the circumstances Shammah faced. Farmers are running toward him from their homes, and you can see the concern and admiration on their faces. Upon reaching Shammah, they begin to help him to his feet, while praising him and patting his back. He alone had saved their livelihood, but he is so tired that he drops to his knees. He thrusts his sword into the ground, lays his hands over the hilt, lowers his head, and exhales as he finally relaxes his body.

The battle has been long and hard, and only a few of the enemy forces had escaped him. The pain in his arms is minor as compared to the fatigue that is overtaking him. He has won the battle, and his name and exploits will be spoken of in homes tonight. The farmers help him up again and lead him to one of the homes on the edge of the field. Shammah is hoping for something to eat and drink, and he is looking for a place to rest.

He is thankful that the Lord had won such a victory for him on this day. Some would be in wonder and awe over the bravery he had exhibited. Others would wonder why anyone would fight so hard over peas!

Well, peas or lentils were used to make pottage, such as the pottage that Jacob fed to Esau in exchange for his birthright. The Hebrew word for "lentil" means "to tend a flock." It is used only four times in the Bible. When David ran from Absolum, men brought lentils to him. Likewise, lentils were food for Ezekiel when he was lying on his side for 390 days. Now we see Shammah fighting for this precious commodity, which provided great sustenance for the poor. Lentils are rich in the proteins that are needed to sustain the body's muscles and blood.

This story takes place during the farmers' harvest time. They had arduously tilled the ground and watched over their plants for months. They had chased away rabbits and birds, as they looked forward to the time of harvest.

Have you ever worked hard for something in anticipation of the day when it would finally become yours? Then, all of a sudden something happens, and the enemy comes to snatch it away. This robs you of your joy, your anticipation, and your caring. You grow very disappointed, for you had been praying, fasting, and seeking God. It looked like things were beginning to flourish and hope was burning in your heart. Now you need a major breakthrough from God.

Maybe the issue concerned your children's salvation or something related to your bills or finances. Perhaps it was about your own spiritual growth or revival in your life or in your church.

We can learn many things from the example of Shammah and the farmers in the pea patch. The farmers had expected that day to be the beginning of their harvest. Then the Philistines appeared at the edge of the field. They had come prepared to take the crop. The Philistines' plan had been to wait until the harvest in order to rob the Hebrews of their peas, leaving them helpless and hungry and under complete bondage to them.

The name of Shammah means "consternation," a condition which leads one to become dismayed, anxious, and amazed. Now, I don't know if Shammah was such a formidable man that he caused consternation in others or if his parents were dismayed at his birth. Whatever the case, he became a man of courage, and he had to overcome many things to become the brave man he clearly turned out to be. He had to overcome his fears and insecurities, and he obviously refused to live up to his name by entering into consternation.

That's the kind of man you want on your team, for such a man has learned how to overcome his fears and his self-life. Such a man has the confidence that is needed to stand alone in the face of all opposition.

His full name was Shammah, the son of Agee, and this appellation is best translated as: "consternation, the son of 'I shall increase.'" Shammah's destiny was to increase in stature, strength, and reputation, and each of us shares this destiny with him. No matter what your background is, you can change your destiny.

FULFILL YOUR DREAM

My father, Dr. G.M. Farley, was the son of a West Virginia coal miner. He grew up in the mountains and as a young man, he followed his father into the mines, where he worked for several years. But my father always had a desire for more. Therefore, he educated himself and went on to preach the gospel across the United States, Canada, and several other nations. He helped to start churches in Nigeria, Philippines, and South America, and he authored several spiritual and secular books. He recorded several country gospel albums, painted and illustrated several magazine and book covers, sold his paintings, and pastored churches.

My father came to a place in his life where he knew he had to make a choice. Would he live in a coal mining town and work in the mines for the rest of his life, or would he fulfill his dream? He chose to fulfill his dream. As a result of his intrepid choice, thousands found Christ as their Savior and many were delivered and healed.

My father persevered and so did Shammah, who was a man of perseverance and follow through! When the enemy decided to steal the harvest, Shammah said, "No!" He was willing to lay his own life on the line for the lives of others.

John Paul Jones bought a merchant ship during the Revolutionary War and armored it as a battleship. In this renovated vessel, he sailed out and met a British man-of-war ship that had 40 guns. They locked in battle, and the big ship fired on them. It soon looked hopeless to the Americans.

Nonetheless, they persevered, and, as they drew closer and got within shouting range, the British admiral said, "Do you yield and surrender?"

John Paul was quick to answer, "I have not yet begun to fight!" Then the Americans fired again on the bigger ship. Soon thereafter, they were able to board the ship and defeat the British!

Similarly, Shammah said, "I'm not running. I'm tired of the enemy stealing my victory. I'm tired of quitting short of success." He didn't even wait for others to join in. There were no reinforcements, and he was outnumbered, but he had God! And he knew that God was all he needed.

Shammah is the kind of man you want to have on your team. Such a man always stands up for what is right and will stay by your side all the way through. He is the kind of leader who won't desert you when things start looking bad, a leader who will say, "I know it looks tough, but I'm with you! Let's see this thing through!"

Too many people who are on church boards today come into leadership with their own agendas, and they are looking for position and power. These leaders are not prepared to meet adversity in the same spirit that was demonstrated by Shammah. Instead, they often become disgruntled and con-fused, and they become defensive and begin to engage in blame-shifting. They will say, "I feel like God wants me to resign," or they may simply walk away. But those who have the spirit of Shammah will stand firm and they will expect God to come through and bring light into the darkness. They will endeavor to back you up and support your vision even in the midst of adversity.

The Shammah-type leader will realize the truth of this Scripture: *"I can do all things through Christ who strengthens me"* (Phil. 4:13 NKJV). This kind of leader will realize the enemy isn't the disgruntled person that may be stirring up trouble, but a true spiritual force in high places—the adversary of the Church of Jesus Christ. And such a leader will know how to engage in spiritual warfare against the true enemy.

Such a leader believes the words of Paul who wrote, *"For we do not wrestle against flesh and blood, but against principalities, against powers, against the rulers of the darkness of this age, against spiritual hosts of wickedness in the heavenly places"* (Eph. 6:12 NKJV).

Shammah fought for the sustenance of the people. It wasn't his fight. It wasn't even his pea patch. The fight wasn't about him; it was about standing against the adversary in behalf of others.

PERSEVERANCE

Perseverance is "the act or state of persisting in anything undertaken; continued pursuit or prosecution of any business, plan or effort." Galatians 6:9 (KJV) says, *"Let us not be weary in well doing: for in due season we shall reap, if we faint not."* In First Corinthians 16:13 (KJV) we read: *"Watch ye, stand fast in the faith, quit you like men, be strong."*

Success does not come to the weak of heart, those who leave or turn aside when the road grows long or hard. It comes to those who hold on to the vision they've been given.

Let's take a look at Jacob's example. Remember the time when he was alone in the dark and was praying? He had sent everyone ahead to meet his brother, Esau. There, while being alone in the darkness, he was accosted by an angel of God. He wrestled with the angel all night long. Jacob would not give up. He was determined to hold on till the end. He would not let go until he received the blessing he was looking for.

This is similar to the stance of King David, who sang: *"My heart is fixed, O God, my heart is fixed: I will sing and give praise"* (Ps. 57:7 KJV).

We could name many Bible characters who showed great perseverance in their life with God. These men and women are heroes of faith and heroes of the Word. They understood that dreams don't happen just because you want them to. They knew you must hang in there and be tenacious, that you must remain steadfast until you finally see the vision come to pass.

What if Daniel had stopped praying for a week? What if Shadrach, Meshach, and Abednego had bowed down to the idol? What if Jacob had stopped wrestling when the angel of the Lord said, "Let me go"?

Jesus said, *"No man, having put his hand to the plough and looking back, is fit for the kingdom of God"* (Luke 9:62 KJV).

SPIRITUAL GROWTH

As believers, we all need leaders on our team who will go the distance to make sure that the Word of God is kept pure. Such a leader is one who will take up your burden when it becomes more than you can handle alone. This type of leader knows that the whole Word of God, not just sections of it, is necessary for nurturing spiritual growth.

It is easy to become what I call "spiritually disproportionate" if we are not careful. We must not overemphasize one truth over others. This does not mean to say that God will not use a man in one gifting or a particular area of faith, such as a deliverance ministry, a faith ministry, or a healing ministry, but it is important for every leader to be well-balanced in spiritual understanding, in his grasp of the entire Word of God.

The main idea is to try and be like Christ as much as possible. Learning from God is like riding down a large river. Each time God wants to teach you something He leads you off into a tributary. During one of these side trips it will seem as if everything that comes into your life deals with a single aspect of the Word. He may be teaching you, for example, about the Holy Spirit or about faith, or about giving. Such times are exciting periods of teaching in which you become fascinated with new insights into your Christian walk.

Eventually, however, you find "the boat" taking you back out into the main river, and you begin to flow with its current until God takes you off into another tributary. We become "disproportionate" when we get stuck in one tributary or one truth and major on nothing but that and then begin calling it our ministry.

Jesus was a deliverance minister, a teacher, a healer, and a prophet. He baptized people in the Holy Spirit and manifested all the gifts of the Holy Spirit. He was an evangelist, an educator, a counselor, etc, and He always stayed true to the whole Word.

Trying to be as complete as possible in ministry is a challenge in our day, because everything has become so specialized. Doctors no longer seem to treat you for all your needs. Instead, they will refer you to a specialist who deals with the part of your body that is hurting.

The church has become similar in many respects. For instance, we may send someone to a man who has a deliverance ministry or we may send another person to a counselor or a faith healer instead of ministering to that person's need ourselves. I've even heard believers saying, "My pastor said we don't have that ministry here, so you'd better try so-and-so."

It is time for us to ask ourselves if God works only through "specialists." Do we need to make an appointment at someone's healing office or at someone's prophecy office? It seems that most of these matters were taken care of for years by the local church, not in specialists' offices. People met the God who could do all things for them at the altar in the front of the church. The pastor would simply share the Word and expect by faith that change would happen through God and His Word.

In those days pastors and leaders would not respond to a need by saying, "That's not my calling, or I just don't feel led." Like Shammah, they knew that their God would supply all our needs, no matter what that need might be, by Christ Jesus. (See Philippians 4:19.)

Just two years ago I watched as God delivered a young man who was living in sin. He had been using cocaine, Ecstasy, heroin, speed, marijuana, tobacco, and liquor. He had been living in fornication with a young woman. Then he came to Christ at an altar in a church service and got up from his knees completely freed from all of those addictions and behaviors. Two weeks later he was married and baptized, and now he is serving God with all his heart!

God did all this as the young man knelt at the altar. No counselors, deliverance ministers, healers, or prophets laid hands on him. The Word went forth, and this young man responded with the faith God imparted to him.

CHAPTER 4

BENAIAH, THE SON OF JEHOIADA

(PRAYER WARRIOR)

EARLY one morning just after dawn, Benaiah was following lion tracks in the snow. The adrenaline rush caused by the hunt had tempered his awareness of the bitter cold; still he found himself wondering how Israel's brutally hot summer season could be transformed into such arctic coldness. Each prodding step he took into the four inches of wet snow was one of caution. Squinting as a result of the bright glare from the pure whiteness, he thought, "Am I being watched by the beast even now?"

The lion had begun stalking the village several days before the snowfall and had ravaged several sheep over the past month. The men of the village had hunted the beast to no avail. They did, in fact, kill a lion, but apparently it wasn't the right one.

Earlier that morning, the lion had grabbed a young girl, Benaiah's niece, as she headed to the well for water. She cried out and her father, Carmi, Benaiah's brother-in- law, ran to help her, only to be wounded by the lion as he tried to grab his daughter.

Benaiah was a fearless man. He, like his father had been, was a valiant man with an impeccable reputation. He had racked up victories by killing two lion-like men, heroes of Moab. Those were fierce fights. Then there was another fight with a spectacular Egyptian man; some said the Egyptian was nearly 7 feet tall. This foreign foe had brandished a spear, but Benaiah was armed with a mere staff. Nonetheless, he rushed at the Egyptian, wrestling the spear from his grip. Then, using his enemy's own weapon, he killed him.

Yes, Benaiah was a brave man. However, instead of hunting lion-like men, he was on the hunt this time for a real lion, a wild beast that was capable of shredding even the most formidable fighting man to pieces.

Anger boiled in Benaiah's heart as he recklessly stomped through the snow. Following the tracks of his niece's killer, he knew he must not turn back until he killed the beast!

Just then a thunderous roar echoed through the snowy morning and halted Benaiah in his tracks, sending a shiver up his spine. The roar was coming from around the next group of rocks. Benaiah raised his spear and eased around the edge of the rocks where he saw a cavernous pit. The lion had fallen into the pit and couldn't climb its way out of the slippery, snow-covered walls.

The beast fixed its gaze upon Benaiah with a murderous stare. They stood motionless for a long time, gazing into each other's menacing glares.

Anger continued to rage in Benaiah's heart, and he jumped into the pit. He thrust his spear into the side of the giant beast. The lion whirled with its enormous body and slung Benaiah off his feet onto the side of the pit.

Turning to face his attacker, the lion glared at Benaiah in anger and pain. Benaiah struggled to his knees and grabbed his short sword in expectation that the lion would soon charge at him. He could see the muscles of its haunches tensing. Then the beast gave forth a mighty roar. It was a roar of unbridled rage, and it was obviously directed right at Benaiah. Immediately thereafter, the beast sprang toward him.

Benaiah jabbed upward with his sword just as the beast leaped for him. He felt the blade connect, and then he was flattened to the ground by the weight of the lion that fell on top of him. He quickly threw his arm upward to grab the mouth of the lion, hoping to defend himself, but it wasn't necessary; there was no more movement. Benaiah's sword had pierced the lion's heart and killed him instantly.

He frantically freed himself from the weight of the carcass and tried to climb the walls of the pit, but Benaiah could not get any traction or find anything to grab on the snow-covered walls. He called out in the hope that someone would hear him, but he was without any reinforcements, because he had left the village in such a frenzy in his zeal to hunt the lion.

He then decided to sit down on the carcass of the lion and wait. Soon he heard a sound coming from the direction from which he had traveled. He called out, the people responded, and they lifted him from the pit. What kind of a man would jump into a pit and face a lion?

My wife, Karren, and I went on our honeymoon 35 years ago during the winter. We stayed in a cabin in the woods at Blackwater Falls State Park high in the mountains of West Virginia. It snowed while we were there, which only served to accentuate the beauty of the forest and park. Early one morning, my wife awakened me with a question: "Rick, what was that?"

I could tell she was nervous, so I asked her what she was talking about, for I had been sound asleep and had heard nothing. "That sound," she said. "It sounds like a baby crying. Now it sounds like a woman screaming!"

This time I heard it, and it was a sound I had never heard before.

Later, we went outside in the snow, and we found tracks near our cabin. We discovered that a mountain lion had been walking around our cabin!

Well, my bride quickly informed me that we were checking out that day. She didn't want to spend one more night in the woods with anything that sounded like that. Just the lion's cry was enough to shake us up. It makes me wonder what kind of man would go into a snow-covered pit armed only with a spear in order to face a lion.

We need lion-killers, for the devil is going about as a roaring lion, seeking whom he may devour. (See 1 Peter 5:8.) Benaiah was a man who said, "I don't care what the circumstances are, I'm going to get that lion!" Many Christians consider themselves to be lion-killers until it snows, then they have another excuse not to go to church.

I have news for you. The lion is always in the pit. The pit is a place into which many will fall in life, whether it is a pit of sickness, finances, confusion, depression, or something else. Just remember, though, the lion is always there, and he's waiting to devour you when you fall into the pit.

When we find ourselves in a pit facing a roaring lion, one thing is for certain. It's either us or the lion. It's either kill or be killed. There can be no escape without a fight.

Last year our local newspaper published a picture of a man who had killed a 420-pound black bear with a bow and arrow. More impressive than that and the thing that amazed me most was the fact that the hunter had only one leg! He had lumbered into the woods on crutches and had faced a bear with a meager bow and arrow. What if he had only wounded the animal and it had charged him? Once he had decided to strike, however, the man was obviously committed to the challenge. There was no running away. That's courage!

Do Battle With Your Lions!

It's time to do battle with your lions! Are you tired of being sick? Are you tired of the devil messing with your finances or robbing you of your blessings? Are you tired of him harassing your family and church and confusing your children? Then you must jump into the pit, grab the lion, and smite him, as Benaiah did. It's the only way to achieve victory, for a victory cannot be won without an earnest fight.

I have often asked myself why the Word tells us that this victory took place *"in the time of snow."* I believe this had a lot to do with the killing of the lion and the courage of the man.

Let's take a look at what Job says about it. Job 38:22-23: *"Have you entered the treasury of snow, or have you seen the treasury of hail, which I have reserved for the time of trouble, for the day of battle and war?"* A treasury of snow? Wow! What has snow got to do with war? This is a spiritual metaphor.

One snowflake will often get "glued" to other snowflakes. So snow can collect like a huge reservoir on a mountain peak and continue collecting there until summer. When it melts, it fills the streams and rivers all summer long. Even in tropical lands, such as South America, and more arid regions, such as California, snow collects in the mountains in the winter and creates the water supply that's needed in the valleys below for the summer months. No snow on the Sierra Mountains means drought in California.

In other words, the snow collects so there will be water for the dry times. Spiritually, a collection of yet-to-be-answered prayers will eventually "thaw out" and water your ministry until fresh rains come. You should have deposited "a treasury of snow" in Heaven for your times of war. This treasury will supply you with what you need to carry on, as you wait for God to answer you in your time of need. Your prayers have been collected in Heaven, and your yet-to-be-answered prayers will begin to flow during the dry times of your life.

You may be asking whether this could be true. Well, let's look at Acts 10:2-4 (NKJV): *"A devout man and one who feared God with all his household, who gave alms generously to the people, and prayed to God always. About the ninth hour of the day he saw clearly in a vision an angel of God coming in and saying to him, 'Cornelius!' And when he observed him, he was afraid, and said, 'What is it, lord?' So he said to him, 'Your prayers and your alms have come up for a memorial before God.'"*

Cornelius's prayers and alms were a memorial in Heaven. That means they were placed in a position of remembrance by God.

This is an intriguing metaphor for what God's Word reveals in the story of Benaiah killing the lion in the time of snow. Snow represents prayer, and prayer produces faith to destroy the lion that comes after you.

Did you ever notice how quiet it often gets when it snows? That's because snow absorbs sound waves and creates a soft and gentle quietness. It may squeak or crunch when you walk on it, but when the temperature gets to be around 40 degrees, those sounds are replaced by the peaceful and relaxing sound of splashing water. Prayer produces peace in your heart when you have to face the lion in the pit. Why? Because you are prayed up, and you have prayed through to victory!

Benaiah was the son of a chief priest in Israel's temple. I believe that is where he learned to be a man of prayer and faith. He was prayed up, and he had prayed through!

I remember one pastor whose church had gone through a split which left the church without the ability to pay his salary. He worked for another ministry at the time, but the loss of nearly half his income really placed him in "the lion's pit." Because of the other ministry, he couldn't work full time and fulfill its requirements. So he and his wife had to rely on prayer and faith in God.

Each month his wife would call him at the church and tell him how much money they needed to pay their bills.

He would always say, "Dear, we still have a couple days left, and God knows what our bills are. It will be ok! For three years this monthly ritual took place. Each month was a financial fight of prayer and faith. The conclusion of his story, as he described it, is, "God never failed, not for even one month!" The peace he had in the midst of his battle with "the lion," was a result of his prayer life and his faith.

Snow is also God's way of cleaning the air and removing impurities. When you pray and allow the Holy Spirit to wash over you, He does the same. He removes the impurities in your life through prayer. Just as snow is able to remove viruses and dust from the air, prayer will help you deal with sin and impurity in your life.

Snow has different consistencies which are dependent on the shape of the snowflakes and the amount of space between them as they fall upon each other. We learned this as children, that some snow is good for making snowmen and other types of snow won't stick together well enough to make anything, not even a snowball!

In a similar vein, God never answers our prayers the same way. Sometimes the Holy Spirit moves in your life in one way and at other times He does something different, depending upon the need and the will of God. God always remains sovereign in the ways He answers our prayers.

He may store some answers for another day. Why? Because God knows when the real need is present, and He knows what the future holds.

HE KNOWS THE FUTURE

I remember a prophecy I received once at a camp meeting. It was about a major financial blessing that would be coming to me. The one who was prophesying this said the blessing would come "shortly." Well, to me "shortly" is likely to be in the next week or next month. However, I found that the meaning of "shortly" to God was different than what I thought it meant. After receiving the prophecy, I started looking for a big blessing, because many of the other things mentioned in the prophecy were accurate and they were about things the speaker could not have known about me. Well, time passed, and I prayed and thanked God, but nothing happened.

Three years later, I learned that I had to have heart surgery. My insurance failed to pay many of the bills, and this left me with a huge deficit. Well, guess what? Suddenly God dropped a blessing on me that covered all of my hospital costs. I had been looking for something I could spend and enjoy, but God was watching the future for me, and He was holding the answer to my prayer until I really needed "the snow from His treasury."

Snow is white, because it contains the full spectrum of light. This is comparable to prayer, which will allow you to bathe in the Presence of Jesus, who is the Light of the World. Your faith will become full because of the assurance of His Presence.

Benaiah went after the lion in the time of snow. He was cleansed by prayer. He had a reserve of God's grace which he knew would be shed upon him. He was bathed in Jesus and in His glorious Presence.

Being prepared to face your lion, and getting ready to battle him require a life of prayer.

One survey of Christian pastors asked this question: "How much time do you spend in prayer each day or week?" While the answers varied, when they were averaged out, the total was shocking. The average was five minutes a day in prayer!

That's a sobering thought that should cause great concern, especially when you consider the fact that the enemy has not weakened his attacks upon the church or its leaders.

If we are going to fight the lion, we need seasons of snow in our lives. For example, I remember a Christian psychologist calling me one day. He worked as a counselor for the state hospital. He had been working with a young woman for about six months, and he stated that he felt he had done all he could for her. He went on to say that he felt she needed prayer and deliverance.

I told him to bring her to the church so we could minister to her need. Then I called my associate minister and my wife and asked them to spend the day before her arrival with me in prayer and fasting for this young woman. The reason the counselor felt his patient needed spiritual help was because of her background. She had been raised in a home of satan worshipers, and she had been sexually molested by every male member of their family as well as the extended family. They used her as a surrogate to produce fetuses for their sacrifices. She suffered from Multiple Personality Disorder and now had 13 different personalities!

This young lady and the psychologist arrived the next day, and we began to minister deliverance to her by casting out each of the demonic personalities individually. Finally, they were cast out and we were able to talk to the young woman herself. (This is not to say that everyone with multiple personalities is oppressed by satan, however.)

I called the psychologist three months later to ask how she was doing. He informed me that she now had a new problem. I asked him, "What's the problem? Is she oppressed again?"

He said, "Oh, no. Her problem now is a good one! She is looking for work, because she has been pronounced 'normal' and cannot draw Social Security anymore!"

Praise God for the power of prayer that came to us as we took time to fight the lion during the time of snow!

During the Second World War, Hitler attacked Russia. The thing that defeated his forces was the brutal Russian winter. The snow and cold destroyed his army.

Benaiah slew the lion in the pit during the time of snow! We read of him on subsequent occasions as a man who stood by David's side.

When David chose to give the kingship to Solomon, one of the men he sent for was Benaiah who was assigned to help protect Solomon. Benaiah then went on to replace Joab as commander of the Army. He remained loyal to David and to David's son, as well.

AN ATTITUDE OF PRAYER

Benaiah shows us symbolically that one of the attitudes you want in the leaders who work with you is an attitude of prayer, an attitude that is found in leaders who know how to reach God's throne in prayer. Such a leader will always bolster you with prayer. You need leaders around you who have a deep relationship with God, leaders who can face the lions because they know it is "the time of snow" in their lives.

Benaiah was a man who seemed to have no fear. Many of the others had killed more men than Benaiah had, yet he was one who took on the greater warriors. An enemy's size made no difference to Benaiah. Whether it was the "lion-like men of Moab" who were very furious in battle, or a 7-foot-tall Egyptian, Benaiah was prepared for the fight. He was a man who would face any problem without regard to how large it seemed. He was a man of prayer, and a life of prayer gives you that kind of confidence and courage!

The kind of leader you need on your team is one who possesses great faith and remains a loyal servant to you. Such a leader says, "We can do this. With God we can handle it." His attitude is: "We can do all things through Christ!" Only a man of prayer, a man who has a deep and abiding relationship with God will be able to produce and maintain this kind of attitude when the lion comes in the time of snow.

CHAPTER 5

ELEAZAR, THE SON OF DODO

(LOYALTY AND COMMITMENT)

THE sounds of fighting fill the air. Men are yelling and screaming in pain, and you hear steel striking steel as the warriors swing their weapons at each other in rage. One by one, warriors are collapsing on the ground. Dismembered bodies litter the barley field. You notice that one side is retreating, for the men of that force have turned to run away. This continues as other men fall and many turn to flee. Soon there are only two men left, and they are surrounded by what is left of an army.

These two seem to show no desire to back down. There is a look of determination on their faces, and there is even the trace of a smile on one man's face. You know him now; it's David, the King of Israel!

King David and his army have marched to Pas-dammim. They had heard that the forces of the Philistines had gathered there, perhaps to take over the barley harvest. When they arrived, they were met by a large group of Philistine soldiers.

It is not long before the Israelites and the Philistines engage in a fierce battle. They fight until the sun is high and the heat of the day beats down upon the two armies. Many in David's army are dead, dying, or fleeing now, and the only reinforcement available to them is a faithful cohort named Eleazar who is standing in the field with David.

Completely surrounded by enemy troops, these two men stand back to back as they strive to defend each other. They don't run, and they don't surrender. They stand steadfastly together, true comrades-in-arms, and they are fighting to protect a field that is sown in barley.

Eleazar and David are on the brink of total exhaustion. Still, they stand their ground and block the seemingly incessant blows of the enemy. The battle rages on, but finally the enemy sees how futile it is to try and take these two valiant men of God. They apparently recognize that God and His supernatural forces are them, and, without doubt, He will defend them, protect them, and give them a great victory!

Eleazar is clearly determined to wield his weapon as long as he has the strength to do so. However, it is growing heavier with each swing, each thrust, and each blow that he blocks. What an amazing thing this is to behold! Two men bravely fighting in the midst of a vast enemy army. People write songs and legends about such heroism.

God is with David and Eleazer and He will give them a great victory! In spite of the odds, they are winning! Many of the enemy forces have fallen. David is fighting as fiercely as Eleazer. Sometimes they're fighting back to back, and sometimes side by side.

Eventually the confidence of the enemy soldiers seems to fade away. David sees this in their eyes and body language, and this causes him to press more vigorously toward them. They finally turn and run for their lives.

The two brave warriors stand their ground and watch in amazement as the Philistines flee from the barley field. They look at each other and sit down, almost collapsing because they are so tired.

David then notices that Eleazer hasn't lain his sword down. He is still gripping it tightly in his hand. His fingers are locked around the hilt of his sword. He has fought so hard and gripped his weapon with such determination that he can't let go! David helps pry his fingers free from the sword. Both are tired as they stand and begin to leave the field. They see other men returning now that the battle is over. These have come to take spoil from the bodies of the Philistines.

GOD HAS HELPED!

Eleazer's name means "God has helped." In his name we see a man of faith who knows where his strength and life come from—from God in Heaven. Here is a man who shows us that in the service of God, we should always keep up our willingness and our resolute spirit and not give in to the weakness and weariness of the flesh.

Like Eleazer, you must pray until the battle is finished and hold onto the throne of God until you know you have broken through and that God has heard and will move in your behalf. These mighty men of David have an attitude of seeing the job through to completion. Be like them; don't ever give up. Believe that God will come through for you.

CATCH THE VISION AND RUN WITH IT!

Catch His vision and run with it, seeing it through to the end even when other people have deserted you in the midst of the battle. Those who are loyal and full of determination will always remain by your side.

Remember how Daniel had asked God for wisdom on a vision, but the answer didn't come right away? Even so, Daniel had set his heart to know and believe God; therefore, he knew that God would eventually come through for him. He continued to fast and pray for 21 days until God sent an archangel with His answer. The enemy tried to hinder and block the answer from coming forth, but Daniel prevailed because he had set his heart to not give up and to believe that God would give him a breakthrough.

During the Olympics in Mexico City, a marathon runner from Uganda pulled a hamstring, then fell and cut his knee. They kept the finish line open for him as he limped along for the rest of the race. When he finally finished the race, reporters ran up to him and asked, "Why didn't you stop?"

He said, "Because my country didn't send me here just to start the race, but to finish it." Like him, we must continue on the race that is set before us while looking unto Jesus who is the author and finisher of our faith. (See Hebrews 12:1-2.)

This is what Israel did in the heat of the battle. The noon day sun was beating down on them. Sometimes they seemed to be winning, but at other times they were being pushed back. It all depended upon one man—Moses! He was told by God to sit on the hilltop and raise his staff over his head. As long as he held the staff aloft, Israel would win. When his shoulders would begin to ache and cramp, however, he would have to lower his arms. What a torture this must have been for him, as he watched Israel's army fight and realized that, as soon as his arms lowered, some of his men would die. I can't even imagine the anguish he experienced in his heart and body as he struggled to keep his arms raised upward toward Heaven.

What Moses needed at that point was an Eleazer! He needed someone who would stand alongside him and fight with him. Moses found his Eleazer in Aaron and Hur. These two men saw the need and stepped up to the challenge. Each one of them took one of Moses' arms and held it up.

This is an example of true teamwork! At our annual county fair there are tractor pulls and horse pulls. One horse can pull 9,000 pounds. This fact might make one think that a team of two horses would pull twice as much—18,000 pounds. Well, when put to the test, the team of two horses didn't pull just double, they pulled 27,000 pounds! This example shows us that one plus one equals three in strength. That's why the Bible says one will put 1,000 to flight, but two will be able to chase 10,000 away.

It is essential to have an Eleazer who will stand with you and be loyal to the end, even in the seemingly little things like the defense of a barley field.

When I was pastoring near Frederick, Maryland, the Spirit began to speak to me about pioneering a church in Martinsburg, West Virginia. I did not know anyone in Martinsburg, so to do this I would have to step out in "blind faith."

After several months of prayer, my family and I went forth in obedience to what we believed God wanted us to do. There was one young man in our church who came to me and said, "I feel God wants me to move to Martinsburg and help you start the church."

So both our families moved and starting looking for a building in this community in West Virginia's Eastern panhandle.

We found an old storefront and began working to fix it up. The young man who had volunteered to help us worked tirelessly. He and I spent every hour in prayer as we worked together. We cleaned, painted, and prayed! As people began to respond to our flyers and advertising, the church began to grow. I soon discovered that my young assistant was a man with a true Eleazer spirit. No matter what happened, he always stood with me.

If he visited in a home and someone spoke against the church or me, he would respond by correcting them. Once, he came to me and said, "I'm not getting enough preaching time."

I said, "Do you realize how many street corners there are in this town that don't have preachers?"

He responded to this idea by taking his guitar and a bundle of tracts to the street corners of our city every Saturday and handing out tracts, preaching, singing, and witnessing to the passersby. He remained loyal to me and stood alongside me in ministry until he was ready to pastor his own church. This young man wanted to serve in whatever ways he could. If he disagreed with me he would tell me, but he never turned against me. Together, we pioneered a church that is still in existence some 25 years later.

LOYALTY AND COMMITMENT

Loyalty and commitment are important leadership qualities. David and Eleazer, as I described in the opening paragraphs of this chapter, were fighting in Pas-Dammin, which means: "The palm of bloodshed." Do you ever feel that you are in "the field of bloodshed," standing against the enemy alone? If so, you need a friend like Eleazer who will stand with you until the battle is over. Remember, Eleazar means: "The Lord is my helper!"

Mark 16:19-20 (NKJV) says, *"So then, after the Lord had spoken unto them, He was received up into heaven, and sat down on the right hand of God. And they went out and preached everywhere, the Lord working with them and confirming the word through the accompanying signs."*

God knows you. Psalm 87 says those who are born in Zion are recorded in His Book. The Bible says that the battle is the Lord's! When Israel was being attacked by the Moabites, Elisha told Israel to dig ditches and fill them with water. When the sun rose in the morning, the ditches appeared to be full of blood. Only God could destroy the enemy with a sunrise.

THE SUPERNATURAL ELEAZAR

Jesus has left us with a "supernatural Eleazar." He is the Holy Spirit, the Comforter, which means He is our constant companion. In fact, the Holy Spirit is "the Walker alongside." What makes us overcomers? Why are we more than conquerors? The answer to both of these questions is found in the realization that the Holy Spirit has come alongside us to help us! And He is always there.

Likewise, there are men and women who have the Eleazer attitude. They are gifted to serve and be loyal. They will give you their commitment and hold to it even in the face of opposition. When others desert you, these helpers will stand with you. These folk are not just followers; like Eleazer, they are warriors, as well. They will walk alongside you and help in whatever ways they can.

CHAPTER 6

JOSHEB-BASSHEBETH, THE TACHMONITE

(DISCERNMENT AND WISDOM)

I MAGINE yourself looking up and watching the birds flying overhead and the puffy, white clouds lazily drifting through the beautiful blue sky. In such a peaceful setting, you almost forget that a great and fierce battle is being waged before your eyes.

It is a day when honor will be won by only a few. As you watch this scene unfolding, you realize it's like a spectacular Hollywood movie. Men are swinging their swords, horsemen and horses are falling, bodies are scattered around, and spears and arrows are flying everywhere, piercing through the armor of many soldiers. Yes, a major battle is being waged on this particular afternoon!

As you scan the field in front of you, you see a man moving with great speed and skill. He captures your full attention. You are amazed to see the agility with which he uses his spear. It reminds you of a Bruce Lee movie. This warrior is surrounded by a group of men who move forward and then step backward quickly to avoid the movements of his spear. The soldier is Josheb-Basshebeth, who is also known as Joshebeam.

About 20 men are lying in front of him, and they are either wounded, or they are dying. If he were fighting for the United States in a war today, Joshebeam would likely be awarded the Congressional Medal of Honor, for he fights so intensely and heroically. When an enemy tries to slip around him he notices him in his peripheral vision, then turns and stabs him. All the soldiers are very busy; each is engaged in his own fight.

Joshebeam stands alone, and a large group of enemy soldiers focuses on him and begins to gang up on him. No matter how many soldiers he fights off or kills, the enemies seem to keep on coming toward him and attacking him. This could well be his last battle. Nevertheless, he continues to fight bravely. Eventually, some men appear on the hillside to his right.

When he catches a glimpse of the new soldiers, he smiles broadly, for he realizes there is new hope. The reinforcements consist of David and his men.

Upon seeing this, the enemy retreats. Joshebeam follows them and strikes down more soldiers as they turn and run away. When the battle is over, Joshebeam (who is also known as Adino) counts the bodies of 800 enemy soldiers who were all killed with his spear. This fact alone earned him the title of the greatest of David's mighty men.

This valiant warrior is Josheb-Basshebeth, and, as I've already pointed out, he has two other names in the Scriptures. He is called Joshebeam, the Tachmonite; and Adino, the Eznite. According to Jewish tradition, two of these names were given to him by David. Just as Christ gave His disciples new names and God changed the names of many men in the Bible, David gave this gallant man two new names.

There isn't much said about Joshebeam/Adino in the Bible, except for one short verse in Second Samuel and another verse in First Chronicles. The one thing we can say about him for sure is that if you see him coming after you with a spear, it is time to run and pray!

KNOW YOUR STRENGTHS AND WEAKNESSES

Adino knew what his talents and skills were. To be a leader you need to know both your shortcomings and your talents. The other mighty men were talented in other areas. For example, Eleazer and Shammah were skilled swordsmen. Benaiah was a great fighter with his staff; he could overcome a giant warrior who was armed with a spear by simply using his staff as a weapon.

The Bible tells us that Israel had 600 men who could throw a stone from a sling with exacting precision. I'm sure there were also those who were skilled with lances, and others could use battleaxes effectively.

The point is that Adino knew his talents and he used them with utmost skill and effectiveness. It's important for you to know what you are good at and to apply yourself to it with all your might.

David knew that he needed men who could do things that he couldn't do. Like every good leader, he built a team around him who could make up for his shortcomings. A good, strong team will always make a leader great. David wasn't afraid to have strong, talented men around him.

Since so little is said about Adino in the Bible, we have to look into the meanings of his names in order to discover the attitudes of his heart.

I have always had the philosophy that there is nothing in the Word of God that wasn't meant to be there, and there is nothing in the Word of God that can't speak to us in vital and personal ways. This is particularly true with regard to the names of individuals. It's amazing to see how people named their children in almost prophetic ways, because the children eventually became what their names implied. For example, we have the name of Jacob, which means "the usurper."

David called Josheb-Basshebeth by the name of Adino, which means "the adorned one." According to Jewish tradition, the name literally means: "like a worm, because he bowed down and crawled in the dust before pious men and scholars." For his heroic deeds, David also called him "Haeoni," which means: "the man who is as strong as a tree."

Joshobeam means two things: "Dweller among the people" and "one to whom the people turn." His other names: "Tachmonite and Hachmonite" are basically the same. They both mean "wise, discerning, and shrewd." So Adino must have come from a clan of wise, discerning men, who were full of wisdom. Most certainly, he was a man of discernment and wisdom.

One attribute that every church or ministry board member needs is the ability to understand the times in which we live. These leaders must be able to use discernment and make wise choices based on their discernment. Such leaders are men and women who have the wisdom to weigh all the facts before they make a decision.

The name of Joshebeam implies that he was a man who the people turned to during times of need. His full name—Joshobeam the Hachmonite—would imply that he was the man the people turned to for wisdom and wise choices.

The name of Josheb-Basshebeth means: "He that sits in the seat," and "Tachmonite" is "wisdom or discernment." So again we see that he was a man the people turned to, because he sat in the seat of wisdom.

David called this great leader "Adino the Eznite." As I said before, "Adino" means "adorned one." "Eznite" means "with a sharp, strong spear." When we put all of these names and their definitions together we see that he was a man of wisdom and discernment who sat on a throne, a leader who the people turned to in their times of need. We see, also, that he is "the adorned one."

The Bible shows us that Adino fought until the job was done. He was an overcomer who fought hard and expected to win the victory. In the Bible, the number eight represents new beginnings or a time of resurrection. Adino killed 800 men; he finished the job and thereby a new beginning could be enjoyed by all.

The Bible tells us that Jesus was the standard God raised up for His people! This truth is declared in both the Old Testament and the New Testament. In Isaiah 11:10 (AMP) we read: *"It shall be in that day that the root of Jesse shall stand for the ensign* [banner] *of the people; to it shall the Gentiles seek; and the rest shall be glorious."*

Isaiah 59:19 (AMP) declares: *"So as a result of the Messiah's intervention they shall* [reverently] *fear the name of the Lord from the West, and His glory of the rising sun. When the enemy shall come in like a flood, the Spirit of the Lord will lift up a standard against him and put him to flight, for He will come like a rushing stream which the breath of the Lord drives."*

Jesus did a complete work on the enemy! The devil is now a defeated foe.

The Psalmist writes: *"Thou has given a banner to them that fear thee, that it may be displayed because of the truth. That thy beloved may be delivered; save with thy right hand, and hear me"* (Ps. 60:4-5 KJV). Jesus is our hope, and He is the ultimate Warrior of God! He has overcome and brought a new beginning to all of those who believe in Him.

During the week when I was writing this chapter I preached a funeral for a young man who had battled leukemia. We had prayed for him for several months, and we believed he was being healed, for his blood had changed, and his body was producing its own red blood cells. The white cell count was falling daily.

We were all rejoicing over his healing when a diabetic stroke took him home to be with Christ. At the same time, a 3-month-old baby was rushed to the hospital, and a woman had a cancerous lump removed from her breast.

HOPE, HOPE, HOPE!

What is a believer to do in such times? There's really only one answer to this question: Hope, hope, hope! We have a Warrior who has declared war on our enemies. He is the greatest fighter in God's army, and He has already conquered the enemy. So don't give up, because things aren't always as they seem!

Abraham and Sarah left Ur full of hope. They didn't know where they were going, but they had an inner confidence that they were under God's guidance.

Joseph, with all of the hardships he had to face, never capsized.

Esther was willing to break Persian protocol and walk into the king's presence.

Why were these people able to accomplish what they did? Because of hope.

We trust in the One who has already fought the fight. He is mightier in battle than us and mightier than all His foes. Though He was outnumbered, He was able to defeat all of His enemies. He is the One who sits on a throne, the One to whom we can always turn in our times of turmoil and need. He is the One who now sits at the right hand of God in both power and position. He is gathering believers unto Himself. He has been made the Captain of our faith, because He was God's mightiest Warrior in battle.

When the enemy comes in like a flood, God will raise up Jesus to be our standard (see Isa. 59:19), and He will send Him like a rushing stream driven by His own breath!

Paul writes, *"Who shall separate us from the love of Christ? shall tribulation, or distress, or persecution, or famine, or nakedness, or peril, or sword? As it is written, for thy sake we are killed all the day long; we are accounted as sheep for the slaughter. Nay, in all these things we are more than conquerors through him that loved us"* (Rom. 8:35-37 KJV).

Let's take a look at some other Scriptures that share victorious truths with us:

Galatians 6:9 (KJV): *"And let us not be weary in well doing: for in due season we shall reap, if we faint not."*

2 Corinthians 2:14 (KJV): *"Now thanks be unto God, which always causeth us to triumph in Christ!"*

Colossians 2:15: *"In this God disarmed the evil rulers and authorities. He shamed them publicly by his victory over them on the cross of Christ."* (The *Full Life Study Bible* says: *"He stripped them of their power to hold men and women captive to the dominion of evil against their will."*)

God has triumphed over all enemies, and this means He is literally leading them in a triumphal procession like a Roman general would parade his captives through the streets of Rome behind his chariot as conquered slaves.

Can you envision the devil and all his demons stripped naked and chained to the chariot of Jesus, then being led before the host of Heaven where they are laughed to scorn? Our "Adorned One," who sits on the right hand of God, has defeated the enemy and given us a new beginning.

He has given us access to the very throne He sits upon, which is a place for the people to turn to in their times of need. (See Hebrews 4:16.)

Every leader needs a second-in-command, one who has the wisdom and counsel and direction that are needed in times of battle, when everyone is fighting their own fights, even when he has his own crises to deal with. Such a man is able to carry a large load, thereby helping others to face their own needs. This special kind of leader is full of wisdom and is open to listen to your story and offer wisdom that applies to your situation.

Every leader needs to have a person on his or her team who will listen to them in confidence and give good advice. This kind of leader is one who has been through many struggles and won his own fights.

That's what Josheb-Basshebeth, the Tachmonite, was for David, and it is what Jesus is for each of us. May Christian leaders everywhere rise up and follow their examples during these challenging and difficult times.

CHAPTER 7

ABISHAI, BENAIAH, AND AN UNKNOWN WARRIOR

(ATTEND TO THE LEADER'S WELL-BEING THROUGH COMPASSION, LOVE, SENSITIVITY, AND LOYALTY)

IMAGINE that it's harvest time in Israel. That means the climate is hot and dry. The nights, however, are balmy and clear. David's men are trying to rest in the cave of Adullam. It's a huge cave, and David has 400 men in there with him. They are running and hiding from King Saul.

David had just recently gone to Gath to hide. Gath was the hometown of Goliath, the giant David had killed as a youth. Because of that victory, David found that he was known by the Philistines who lived there, so he pretended to be insane and was able to escape.

The ancient world considered insanity to be an evil sign. The insane were exempt from harm unless their gods became angry with them. Therefore, David was let go and now he and his men have taken refuge in this large cave.

Adullam, where the cave was located, was about 20 miles southwest of Jerusalem and about ten miles from Bethlehem, David's hometown. His family has heard that he is there and they have all come to hide with him in fear of King Saul.

David is very distressed during this particular night. He has his pen in hand, and he is writing the thoughts of his heart to God. Someone has killed a large buck with his bow and arrow, and the venison is roasting over the open fire in the mouth of the cave. The sweet smell of the meat is starting to fill the air in the cave.

Everyone is sitting around swapping stories, as they wait on the meat to finish cooking. David, for now, has placed his sleeping mat near the mouth of the cave. He is watching the sky and contemplating his life story.

It all began when Samuel came to David's home and poured oil on his head. He had declared that David was God's anointed king, the one who would replace Saul.

Now, however, it looked like everything was going in a different direction, for David was hiding in a cave with his family and his men, and they were running for their lives!

This is because they know that Saul has determined to end David's life.

All these people that have come to David in the cave are in distress or in debt, and they are all very discontented. They want him to be their leader. Knowing this causes David to meditate on his situation and theirs, and he begins to write a Psalm. The cry of his heart is:

I cry out to the Lord with my voice; with my voice to the Lord I make my supplication. I pour out my complaint before Him; I declare before Him my trouble. [Obviously, David is not feeling very positive or great at this moment.] *When my spirit was overwhelmed within me, then You knew my path. In the way in which I walk they have secretly set a snare for me. Look on my right hand and see, for there is no one who acknowledges me. Refuge has failed me; no one cares for my soul. I cried out to You, O Lord: I said, 'You are my refuge, my portion in the land of the living.*

Attend to my cry, for I am brought very low; deliver me from my persecutors, for they are stronger than I. Bring my soul out of prison, that I may praise Your name; the righteous shall surround me, for You shall deal bountifully with me' (Psalm 142 NKJV).

David is very depressed at this moment. He stops his meditation as he hears the sounds of laughter breaking out around the fire. Someone is cutting meat and distributing it to hungry people. Abishai has been over in the corner, away from the fire watching David. He notices his leader staring out of the cave's entrance and speaking quiet words as he writes. Abishai can tell that their leader is in a melancholy mood, because he had been around his uncle David on many different occasions.

He takes notice of David getting up and walking toward the fire to get some of the venison. Everyone seems to be lifted in their spirits by the warm food. Some of David's family brought fig cakes, as well. Life is just a little better at this particular moment. David receives his share of meat and sits down to eat with the others.

David's father and mother are both there, and this leads him to think of the "good old days," when the only responsibility he had was to watch the sheep as they grazed. David then looks at his father and says, "Boy, I would give anything to have a drink from that well in Bethlehem. That was the best tasting water in Israel, especially on a hot day, after shepherding all day."

His father gave a knowing smile to his son.

Abishai continues to observe David and he overhears him as he muses aloud about drinking water from the well at Bethlehem. David's nephew then gets up and quietly walks over to where Benaiah and another man are sitting. He shares his concern about the mood of their leader and suggests that they could lift his spirits if they went to Bethlehem and brought a drink from the well to David. The other two agree that this would be a great adventure and a good idea. Benaiah says, "It sure would be a lot better than sitting around in this cave hiding from Saul." The three men know, as well, that this would be a great surprise for their beloved leader, David.

So they quietly make their way to the mouth of the cave and disappear into the night. No one notices because David's parents have brought David's harp with them, and everyone is listening as David sings the new psalm he has just written.

Abishai and the others make their way southwest toward the town of Bethlehem. It takes awhile for them to get to the area surrounding Bethlehem. It is a bright summer night with a moon that's nearly full. The men move stealthily, because they know Bethlehem has a garrison of Philistine soldiers who are encamped there.

When they encounter the first Philistine guard, he has his back toward them, and he is walking in the opposite direction. Abishai silently signals to Benaiah to move to an outcropping of rocks. Benaiah creeps as close as possible to the rocks without being seen or heard and he waits there in silence.

As the guard returns and passes near his position, Benaiah strikes him from behind. The other two run forward and begin to make their way quietly toward the gate of the town, heading toward the well. They wait silently in the shadows of a house, watching three soldiers who are sitting by the well casting lots in the light of a small oil lamp. Benaiah looks at the others and gestures toward the three Philistines.

Abishai shakes his head; there is just too much open space between them and the men. Do they rush forward and attack swiftly or leave empty-handed? Just then, the small lamp begins to flicker; it looks as if God is with them on this night. The lamp is running out of oil, and one of the three gamblers curses as the lamp flickers and its flame dies. The three men stretch and stand, then they walk off toward a building across the square. Abishai and the two others wait a few minutes until the sounds within the house settle down; then they move cautiously over to the well.

Shammah grabs his empty water bag and lowers it into the well. It soon bubbles full and they turn to leave. The night is about spent by the time they arrive back at the cave. They are challenged as they approach the entrance; someone has set a guard near the cave, but they identify themselves and they are granted access.

The sound of the guard's challenge awakens several within the cave, including David, who stirs as the three men enter the mouth of the cave. He immediately recognizes them and notices that they all have sheepish grins on their faces. David begins to wonder what mischief these three warriors could have gotten into without his knowledge.

They approach David, and one of them hands him the water bag. David is obviously puzzled and they grin at him with pride. Abishai says, "I overheard you speaking about how great a drink of water from the well at Bethlehem would taste. So we set out for Bethlehem and returned with your water, fresh from the well in the center of town."

A look of surprise and astonishment crosses David's face, and he expresses humble gratitude to his men. If you were watching closely, you could have seen tears filling his eyes.

ARE YOU CLOSE TO THE KING?

Let me ask you, are you close enough to your King to hear His heart's desire? You may not be able to kill 800 with a spear, but can you get a cup of water?

I recently read a story in our organization's *Spirit* magazine[1]. about a covenant that was written by a young African pastor. It said,

> "I'm a part of the fellowship of the unashamed. I have Holy Spirit power. The dye is cast. I have stepped over the line. The decision has been made. I'm a disciple of His. I won't look back, let up, slow down, back away, or be still. My past is redeemed, my present makes sense, my future is secure. I'm finished and done with low living, sight-walking, small planning, smooth knees, colorless dreams, tamed visions, mundane talking, cheap living, and dwarfed goals.

> I no longer need preeminence, prosperity, position, promotions, or popularity. I don't have to be right, first, tops, recognized, praised, regarded, or rewarded. I now live by faith, lean on His presence, walk by

patience, live by prayer, and labor by power. My face is set, my gait is fast, my goal is Heaven, my road is narrow, my way is rough, my companions are few, my Guide is reliable, my mission is clear. I cannot be bought, compromised, detoured, lured away, turned back, deluded, or delayed. I will not flinch in the face of sacrifice, hesitate in the presence of adversity, negotiate at the table of the enemy, ponder at the pool of popularity, or meander in the maze of mediocrity. I won't give up, shut up, let up, until I have stayed up, stored up, paid up, prayed up, preached up for the cause of Christ. I am a disciple of Jesus. I must go on till He comes, give till I drop, preach all I know, and work till He stops me. And when He comes for His own, He will have no problem recognizing me, for my banner will be clear."

This powerful statement of faith was tacked on the wall of his house, and it was found after he died as a martyr for the cause of the Gospel of Jesus Christ.

The three men who went to get water for their king risked everything. This shows how much their leader had inspired them. It reveals how greatly they admired and valued their leader, so much so, in fact, that it gave them pleasure to risk the greatest of hazards in his service.

This was true loyalty—loyalty of the heart. They must have known that David wouldn't be able to reward them, for there were no external advantages to be had. This reminds me of the disciples of Christ who were completely loyal to Him. What are you willing to risk in His service? Are you willing to suffer for Him if need be?

Take a look at Paul and his history. He was stoned, shipwrecked, marooned, imprisoned, hungry, bitten by a snake, and mocked, but he didn't leave the ministry.

Why do so many leave the ministry today? I'm sure it has something to do with levels of loyalty and commitment—the first principle found in followers of great leaders.

ABOVE FEAR!

Second, it's obvious how little these three men feared the enemy, the Philistines. They actually seemed to be glad to have an opportunity to defy the enemy. I once had a pastor say to me, "I leave the devil alone and he leaves me alone."

Well, that may work in high school with the local bully, but it doesn't work with the devil. He is moving about like a roaring lion, and he is seeking whom he may devour. If he crosses your path and you try to ignore him, you may get eaten!

The Philistines were a people who moved around from place to place tying to occupy other people's territory. They were migratory nomads. This depiction sounds a lot like satan and his forces today; they are going to and fro, and they are seeking whomever they may devour. We must be vigilant at all times.

These three servants of David were just waiting for their lord to express a desire for something. Their attitude was wonderful. In their hearts they said, "No matter what it is, we'll get it for you, and we'll fight the devil all the way!"

GREAT SENSITIVITY

Third, these warriors showed great sensitivity. They felt they had heard the desire of their leader's heart. We are greatest at serving God when we are giving of ourselves to others as they did.

In Luke 19:2-5 (NKJV), Jesus shows us the importance of sensitivity in ministry: *"Now behold, there was a man named Zacchaeus who was a chief tax collector, and he was rich. And he sought to see who Jesus was, but he could not because of the crowd, for he was of short stature."*

The rest of the story is that Zacchaeus ran ahead and climbed up a tree so he could see above the crowd and catch a glimpse of Jesus. Before long, the crowd came down the lane toward the tree he had climbed. When Jesus reached that area, He looked up and saw Zacchaeus. He said, *"Zacchaeus, make haste and come down, for today I must stay at your house"* (Luke 19:5 NKJV).

What does this show us about a leader's ministry? Jesus was always aware of the needs of the people! He knew Zacchaeus' need even though a tremendous crowd was all around him and pressing in upon Him. I'm sure they were pushing and shoving, and many must have been calling out to get His attention. In spite of all this, He could still see the need of Zacchaeus.

There are cries of our hearts that seem to be only heard by God at times, because people around us are not sensitive enough to understand what we are going through and what we need. A leader needs to be sensitive to the cries of his people's hearts.

Normally, we might not expect soldiers and warriors to be sensitive by nature. These three of David's men, however, were team players who were tuned into their leader's heart, and they were sensitive to his needs.

With regard to Zacchaeus, those around the tree, if they noticed him at all, simply saw a short tax collector. To them, in all likelihood, he was a crook, someone they may have even regarded as a wealthy traitor. But Jesus saw a lonely man who had no real friends. He saw a man with needs and hurts, a man who wanted to see Him and was willing to overcome any obstacle to do so!

Such sensitivity contains the capacity to respond to human needs. Blind Bartimaeus cried out for Jesus' help, but his friends told him to keep still and not bother the Master. What did Jesus do? He told them to bring him to Him!

Sensitivity is needed in our jobs, our churches, our homes, and especially in our leadership. We need to learn how to "be there" when our brother or sister needs us. We need to know how to respond by doing more than just saying, "I'll pray for you."

The Holy Spirit will help you really care as though another's person's need were your own. Sensitivity is love extended, and it is not quick to run away from another's problem and need. Sensitivity never shuts out the heart cry of a person in need. Instead, it takes time to listen, to understand, and to comfort.

Jesus made Himself available to people. Zacchaeus was not a governor or a mayor; he was a thief in a tree. The cross on which Jesus was crucified was only a few days in the future. If anybody ever had a good reason to say, "Don't bother me now; I have my own personal problems," it was Jesus in light of all He knew He had to face in the near future. However, He wasn't thinking of Himself at that point. Rather, He saw the need and was sensitive to it.

A lot of people are "on hand," but they are not truly ready to serve. Jesus didn't care if the person's need was convenient or inconvenient. He was sensitive and compassionate. Sensitivity is being available to the cry of someone else's need. What a great attitude or attribute for all people in leadership to have.

Now, let's go back to the cave where David and his men were hiding. What happened after his three warriors brought the water from the well to him was a shock to everyone who was present in the cave. David poured the water on the ground unto the Lord! Then he said, *"Be it far from me, O Lord, that I should do this: is not this the blood of the men that went in jeopardy of their lives? Therefore he would not drink it"* (2 Sam. 23:16 NKJV).

SEEK FIRST TO HONOR GOD

A believer should always seek first to honor God! David respected the courage and the sacrifices his men were willing to make on his behalf. He even equated the water to their blood, which He valued so highly. The blood and life belong to God. Water gained at so great a risk was too valuable for his own drinking, so he gave it to the One they all loved and respected. He gave the precious water to God.

David denied his own desires for self-indulgence. As leaders, we must do the same. We must put to death all desires for personal glory and honor. A leader must not get hurt or mad when he or she isn't praised.

David's purpose was to honor God and give Him all the glory. He also showed us that we should value the things that have been left to us by warriors of the past. The Gospel of Jesus Christ has come to us at great peril. Countless thousands have lost their lives for its sake. Now, we are entrusted with it!

David showed us how much he regarded the lives of those who served with him and how much he valued their loyalty and commitment. He could have taken glory from this and received their sacrifice. Instead, however, he shared the glory with them and showed his regard and appreciation for their actions on his behalf.

The Lord Jesus promises you that your service to Him (and others), even if it is giving a prophet a drink of water, will not go unnoticed and unrewarded.

David regretted expressing his desire for water from the Bethlehem well, because doing so had put his warrior's lives in danger. A leader needs to be constantly aware of what he is saying and how his words might affect others. Sometimes, one's words can bring serious consequences in the lives of others.

David was a man who always endeavored to guard his words. He had asked God to put a guard before his mouth. When we take a close look at the Psalms he wrote, we see that there were low times in his life when he poured out his heart to God. Most of the time, however, David seemed to be a dedicated worshiper and a positive person.

Positive people inspire others! Even when David had the opportunity to be honored and ministered unto, He chose first to honor those who served him. He could have said, "Well, I'm the leader here and I deserve this honor. After all, I have faced great obstacles and many don't understand me and the hardships I endure for God." I'm so thankful for David's example of a leader who was positive and not selfish—one who cared about the needs of others.

Another positive leader was Samson. In his battle with the lion we see an illustration of why being positive is important and effective. Samson was on his way to visit his girlfriend when he was surprised by a young lion. It charged him, and the Spirit of the Lord came upon him, enabling him to rip the lion's jaws apart. With God's help he was able to kill the beast.

Samson did not tell anyone about the incident. Later, when he was traveling with his parents to arrange his wedding, he went to the spot where the lion's carcass lay. A hive of honeybees was using the lion's remains for their place to store honey. Seeing this, Samson took honey out of the mouth of the lion and shared it with his parents, but, still, he did not tell his parents that it had come from the mouth of a lion he had killed.

Certainly, Samson could have told his parents about the horror of the lion attack. He could have described the sharpness of the lion's teeth, how close they had come to his throat, and even how the breath of the lion smelled as it breathed on him while trying to tear his body to pieces. It would certainly have made for an exciting tale. Instead, however, Samson simply shared the sweetness of the experience by giving them honey. In doing so, he was being very positive.

Sometimes we dwell on the fierceness of the battle instead of the sweetness of the victory. Sharing positive things always has real healing effects on listeners. A leader cannot afford to emphasize his or her bad experiences. He does not need to tell others about negative experiences in former churches, does not need to discuss what the devil did, or anything else of a negative nature. Doing so causes fear, distrust, anxiety, and bitterness in others' lives. God tells us to rejoice in our trials.

A positive attitude about the hard places of life will bless others and nourish your own spirit. God has the power to turn hard places into sweet places. Realizing this, quit calling others to complain. Don't feel sorry for yourself, and quit shifting the blame to others.

There are 56 references to honey in the Scriptures. One of these is found in Psalm 19:10, which tells us that *"the Word of the Lord is much sweeter than honey."* In Proverbs

24:13 (NKJV) Solomon gives this command: *"My son, eat honey, because it is good."* Honey is considered to be a blessing from God. His Promised Land flowed with milk and honey.

Honey speaks to of us sweetness and being positive. Sharing the positive will bring life, restoration, health, and healing, as honey does.

Honey can be used to restore energy in someone who is suffering from fatigue, for it is assimilated rapidly into the body and has the power to rejuvenate an individual. It is often used to feed those in famine-stricken regions when their bodies can't digest food any longer. It gives nutrients to the body and inhibits the growth of microorganisms. Likewise, it is used on burn victims to help heal the skin, because it disinfects.

There are 181 known substances in honey. These include amino acids, enzymes, vitamins, 11 minerals, organic acids, glucose, and many others. It is a blood-builder and a quick source of energy. It produces hemoglobin which strengthens the blood and the heart.

Yes, honey is good for the body, but positive thoughts are good for every part of your life—your mind, soul, spirit, and body. The power of life and death is in your tongue. (See Proverbs 18:21.)

David's attitude ministered to those who followed him and so did Solomon's. Follow their example, and share "the honey," not the lion! Tell about the sweetness, not the bitterness. Tell of God's power working in your life; it will build strength in you and those you share it with.

Abishai was a warrior who killed 300 men in battle. He was neither a novice to warfare nor a newcomer to David's camp. He had exhibited his bravery on numerous occasions.

On one of those occasions Saul was chasing David who hid in a cave with his men. While Saul slept, David asked for two volunteers to go with him into the camp of his pursuer; Abishai was the first to step forward.

When they had slipped into the enemy's camp, they made their way to Saul, who was sleeping on the ground. Abishai offered to slay Saul for David right there, but David stopped him. At that point, he took Saul's spear and water bottle, then they slipped out of the camp and over to the hillside.

Next, they called to Saul and showed him his spear and water bottle, noting that they had spared his life.

On another occasion, Abishai was in a battle against the Syrians. His brother Joab was fighting with him when they were attacked by the children of Ammon. Joab said to Abishai, "You take part of Israel, and I will take this part. I will fight the Syrians, and you and your men will fight the Ammonites. If you see me doing poorly against the Syrians, come and help me, and if I see that you are doing poorly against the Ammonites, I will come and help you, and God will be with both of us." With such positive thoughts and expectations, and with the help of God, they defeated both the Syrians and the Ammonites.

Abishai also went forth with the army of Israel and conquered the Edomites in the valley of Salt, where he and his army killed 18,000 Edomites. They established garrisons in Edom, and the Edomites became David's servants.

Abishai also saved David's life in later years, as the king went to war with the Philistines and grew faint in the battle. This is when one of the giants tried to kill David. Abishai did not hesitate to jump in and save David's life. At this point the men of Israel asked David to stay home lest he be killed and they would lose the light of Israel.

We see in these stories that Abishai's attitude as a leader of men and a follower of David, was constantly one of loyalty and sacrifice. He was a committed man, not only to David but to David's vision.

Abishai and men like him leaders who exhibited bravery, faith, wisdom, love, commitment, and loyalty, made David the great king he came to be. David always gave respect and credit to his men and never regarded himself as being better than them. He fought in the same battles alongside them. Then, when the time came that he couldn't fight any longer, they defended him.

ENDNOTE

1. *Spirit Magazine*, Messenger Publishers P.O. Box 850 Joplin, MO August 1998.

CHAPTER 8

A GREAT LEADER REPRODUCES HIMSELF THROUGH HIS TEAM

(DAVID, GIANT KILLER # 1;

AND ABISHAI, GIANT KILLER # 2)

IT is spring in Israel and everything is green. David is lying under the shade of a tree, gazing lazily at his sheep in the field. He has found one of his favorite spots beside a softly flowing stream from which his sheep can drink. The grass is green and tall, and the sheep can feed here all day long.

Every now and then the young shepherd calls a sheep over by name and caresses it, then he sends it back to the flock. His slingshot is close by in case he needs it for a bear or lion. He is about 20 years old, the youngest of his father's children. The others had gone off to war with King Saul, and David was left to watch the sheep.

That he had to remain behind had really upset David at first, for he had wanted to go and fight with the other men, but his father had said no, explaining that his job was to watch the sheep. His father told him that it was the job of men to go forth to war.

David protested just a bit by reminding his father (Jesse) that he had killed a lion and a bear; therefore, he should be allowed to fight for the king. David must have been thinking, "Where was the glory in 'babysitting' sheep?"

He watches the horizon for any sign of wolves or lions, but only sees the clouds gently crossing over the hilltops as they drift through the blue sky. He hears a movement behind him and springs to his feet, grabbing his sling and reaching for a stone. Then he hears a giggle and sees his sister. She tells David that his father, Jesse, wants him at home. One of the servants had been sent to take David's place with the sheep.

When David gets home, his father calls him over and tells him that he wants to send some supplies to his brothers who are on the front lines. He has some fresh baked bread, cheese, and corn for them.

David starts out early in the morning; he is leading a donkey that is laden with supplies. As he heads toward the front, he is really feeling anxious and eager, for he knows he will finally get to see his first battle. When he arrives, he finds everyone sitting on the hillside, looking out over the valley of Elah. Some are in a trench; they are holding their positions against the enemy.

David runs into the army and begins to look for his brothers. While he was talking to a man, he heard a booming voice calling out. The Philistines have sent forth their champion warrior, and he is calling out for someone to fight with him. While he was issuing this challenge, the men of Israel turned and ran in fear, for this man was huge!

His name was Goliath and, according to some, he stood 9 feet tall! He was a well-built man, and his armor with its coat of mail, helmet, sword, shield, and spearhead weighed nearly 300 pounds. He must have been a very formidable foe, indeed. One thing is for certain, he had struck fear in Israel's army.

The giants in our lives, no matter what they may be, always rule through intimidation. You know, fear comes by hearing, just as faith comes by hearing.

Every day Goliath would step out before the Israelites. Every day He would be decked out in his thick, impenetrable armor. Every day Israel's soldiers hid in their trenches, because they were afraid to face him. He would call them names, chide them, and brag about his great prowess.

INTIMIDATING GIANTS

It's the same with our giants today. They evoke fear in our hearts through intimidation. This fear may come in the form of messages in your mind which tell you that you can't do something, or that you don't have enough education, or that people will never accept what you have to say, or that there just isn't enough money. These nagging thoughts may continue in the form of questions: What if you falter? What if you are left alone in this venture? What if the board deserts you? Did you see the looks on their faces when you proposed this project? Whatever your giant is, he has a compete list of intimidating words, doubts, fears, and questions for you.

In this situation, however, David asked some soldiers what was going on, and he questioned, "Why is everyone running from this Philistine?" One soldier told him that Saul had offered a reward to the man who would agree to fight this giant. He even promised to give his daughter to the one who accepted this challenge and to enrich him from his own treasury and to make his family free from taxes in Israel!

David's brother Eliab came over, and he looked really angry. He turned to David and said, "I know why you came down here to spy on the battle. I know your pride and the naughtiness that is in your heart."

David responded, "What have I done now? Isn't there a cause to fight for?"

Someone soon told King Saul about David and his inquires, and he accepted David's offer to fight the giant. David had heard rumors of Saul's fear of Goliath, and how everyone was saying, "What do you fight a giant with, but the tallest man in Israel? Who is the tallest man in Israel? It is Saul!"

Saul tried to get David to wear his armor. In this way he might, after all, get a little credit for the fight. If David wore his armor, he could say, "David would have never won without my fine armor."

Have you ever noticed how people will sometimes try to get you to wear their armor? I remember a particular lady who was in our church years ago. She would sit in the back of the sanctuary, and every time I would preach something that she disagreed with, she would shake her head no. After a while I got to the point where I couldn't even look in her direction when I was speaking. She was trying to get me to fit into her mold, or "wear her armor."

In such situations we need to be like David who said, "No, I don't know how to use this stuff, so I will go with what I know works."

David took his sling and went to a nearby stream to get some smooth stones that would work well with his sling. He picked out five of these river rocks and put them into the bag that was hanging at his waist.

Laughter came forth from the Philistine camp as the opposing forces saw young David walking toward Goliath. What a picture this is: the giant Goliath stood about 4 feet taller than David! Goliath began to laugh at and ridicule David by saying that it is an insult to send a boy to face a man in battle. He then promised he would kill David quickly.

David is standing before the giant now, totally lost in his opponent's shadow. He reaches into his bag and takes hold of a stone, just as Goliath reaches for his large sword. David runs toward the Philistine, and quickly slings the stone toward him. It flies forth with great velocity and hits Goliath in the forehead. The giant is knocked unconscious by its force.

Next, David runs toward the giant and lifts up his sword. With great effort, the lad raises the large sword over his head and brings it down with all of his might across Goliath's neck. With one slash of the sword the giant's head is completely severed from his body.

When the Philistine army saw this and realized that their champion had fallen, they turned and ran away. The forces of Israel charged across the field in hot pursuit of their enemies.

Until this victory, Israel had never had a giant-killer in its midst! David stepped forward in faith and courage and faced the Giant without fear. This must have been quite an inspiration to the men of Israel. I would imagine that the story was told and retold around the campfires that night, and David's fame must have spread throughout Israel and all over the world.

What does a leader with such amazing talent do? He takes what he knows and trains those he leads. I have often heard it said that a shepherd begets other shepherds and sheep beget sheep. David was a man who instilled in his followers the faith and ability to slay their own giants instead of depending on him to be their giant-killer.

Several of David's men are listed as being among his thirty mighty warriors without much being said about their specific accomplishments. All we know about them is their names and the place they hold in history as the mighty men of David.

Abishai was one of those who learned giant-fighting skills from David.

In Second Samuel 21:16-17 we read about a giant named Ishbi-Benob. He was very much like Golaith, a huge man who had a spear that weighed nearly 12 pounds. He had a new sword, as well, and he planned to kill David since he had seen David become faint and weakened in battle due to aging and battle fatigue.

This giant's name means: "the dweller on the mount," and his name reminds us that many of our "giants" in life are found in "high places," and many of these "giants' are idols that must be cast down. They may take the form of money, clothes, or different symbols of pride, status, and esteem. Such things do become true giants in our lives.

David taught his men how to cast down the things that take priority in our lives and usurp the place that only God should have over us. Now that the aging king had been forced to stay home from battle, the men were left to face the giants on their own.

I'm sure David was glad that Abishai had grown in faith to the point where he could now step forward in leadership. I can just imagine what it must have been like to be so tired that you had to lean on your sword. The warfare had been constant and draining.

What must it have been like for David at this point? He realized that he couldn't battle as long and hard as used to be able to do. Then this huge man came toward him. Ishbi-Benob was massive and tall, and others quickly got out of his way. Those who made the mistake of standing against him were quickly dispatched by his strength and prowess.

Now think of what you might do in that situation. You realize the enemy has made you his target. He wants to kill you! His goal is to put an end to your ministry and leadership.

So you raise your weapon, but it is very difficult for you to do so. Nonetheless, you resolve in your heart to go down fighting. Then, suddenly, one of your trusted men steps between you and the giant. Now all you can do is watch and pray as he fights for his life and yours. He is showing great courage and faith, just like you would have done. He seems to have no fear of the giant's size, and he soon delivers a final blow to the enemy.

This must have been David's experience on that day, and he must have realized that he had just watched the next generation of giant-killers. This giant was dead instead of David, because David has instilled the necessary attitude and skills into his men, the valiant members of his team. In a very real sense David had reproduced his life in them.

Realize Who Your Source Is

Abishai's name means "the source of wealth." His name shows us that the way to defeat your giants is to realize who your real source of wealth is. God is your source and your supply. We read in Isaiah 57:15-16 that God dwells in a high place. The word "place," as we see it here, is the Hebrew word yad; it means "a hand, an open hand indicating power, means and direction."

God dwells in a place of power, means, and direction, and His hand is always open for His children. Power is strength.

I remember watching a weight lifter working out in the gym I used to attend. He was 6 feet, 4 inches tall, and he weighed 275 pounds.

This guy could leg press 1,000 pounds, and easily do curls with 100-pound weights. There is great power associated with such strength.

Almighty God lives in the power of authority, and He commands innumerable angels. He created the universe with His Word, and He created light when there was nothing but darkness. God dwells in this place of strength. He is all-powerful.

God has everything that is necessary to overcome the giant named Ishbi-Benob and any other giant, for that matter. We need to put our trust in His strength.

The enemy tries to get us to focus on gaining self-esteem from our position or our work. Though you may fight your flesh, it's important to know that flesh cannot conquer flesh. It's very hard to try and deliver ourselves. In fact, it's impossible to do so. Most of us have tried and we always end up frustrated, but never free.

Determination is good, the desire to be free is good, and discipline is good, but without the inner strength of God, it's impossible to find your way to spiritual freedom. God wants to be your source of strength just as He was for David, Abishai, and all of David's mighty men.

GOD DWELLS IN THE MEANS

God dwells in the means! The means is "the medium, method, or instrument by which some end is accomplished." If you were to ask an architect what his or her greatest needs are, he or she would likely reply that the greatest needs are the intellect, experience, creative ability, and knowledge of architecture. These are what he or she needs to be a successful architect.

Always remember that God has the means to provide whatever you need in life, for you are His child and He loves you with an everlasting love. Whether your need is healing, finances, wisdom, food, clothes, or anything else, God has the strength to deliver you or carry you, and all the means to do so are at His disposal.

THE PLACE OF DIRECTION

God also lives in the place of direction. He knows where He is going and the direction in which He wants you to head. You cannot surprise Him.

Many people lack purpose in their lives. They feel empty and don't know whether they are coming or going. Never forget that God has a purpose for your life, and He has a perfect plan. Indeed, He has everything that is necessary to meet your needs in order to fulfill His plan, and He has the power that's needed to carry you to the end.

CHAPTER 9

SHIBBEHAI, GIANT KILLER # 3

THE next giant was Saph. He was killed by Shibbehai, who was also known as Mebunnai. Shibbehai was listed among the 30 mighty men in David's great team. The name of Saph means "the preserver." This giant represents false security.

When I was in the hospital in 1996, there was a man in the bed next to mine who had regularly run five miles every day and had eaten very conservatively. As I lay in the bed next to him, I listened as the doctor telling him he needed an angioplasty due to the cholesterol that was blocking his arteries.

This wasn't a happy day for him or me, because I was receiving the same news at roughly the same time. While taking care of yourself is a good idea, it is possible to develop a false sense of security about your health from certain health practices, such as jogging, working out in the gym, eating certain foods, and trying to "stay young" by whatever means.

The same thing can be true in the spiritual realm, because there is no substitute for being right with God and having a strong personal relationship with Him. We may think everything will be all right if we just belong to the right church, for example, when this might actually be just a false sense of spiritual security.

There are so many today who have their faith in things other than their relationship with God. The amount of money you have in the bank or your retirement funds are not proofs of God's love.

So many people live in these kinds of "comfort zones" and still go to bed worried about anything that might change their circumstances.

A man once told me that he couldn't really commit his life to God completely because he feared God might make him give up what he had accumulated and call him to be a missionary or preacher. Too many people think, "I'm saved, and that's enough. I give God my hour and some of my money each week."

JEHOVAH IS INTERVENING

Shibbehai, however, did not have a false sense of security. He destroyed the giant through the power of Almighty God. In fact, another translation of his name means "Jehovah is intervening." He knew that God would intervene on his behalf.

This is one of life's greatest lessons: Learning that God will always go before you and knowing that He will always intervene in your life when it is necessary for Him to do so.

I can remember something that happened to me years ago when I was a teenager. A really big bully came up to me and said he wanted to fight me. I looked at him and knew I didn't stand a chance, for I weighed about 135 pounds and his weight was probably more like 250 pounds.

He challenged me by saying, "Come on, I'll give you the first punch. Hit me anywhere."

I looked him in the eye and said, "The Bible teaches me that I should not fight."

Well, at that point in the conversation he started to shove me and say, "Come on! Hit me!"

I repeated my defense once more, but it didn't look like it was going to get me out of my situation. A whipping seemed inevitable!

Then one of his buddies who was standing by his car, walked over and stepped between us. He pushed the bully away. Then he made him apologize to me for trying to start a fight with me.

The truth is I was never happier to have someone intervene on my behalf.

God intervenes in our behalf and fights our battles for us. He defeats our enemies and always helps us. As we have pointed out, the name of Shibbehai means "Jehovah is intervening," and this is what enabled him to slay the giant. Let God intervene in your life and slay all your giants, as well.

CHAPTER 10

ELHANAN, GIANT KILLER # 4

ELHANAN, the son of Dodo of Bethlehem, slew the brother of Goliath. The staff of this giant's spear was like a weaver's beam. Elhanan's name means "the mercy of God, or God is gracious."

The name of Goliath, on the other hand, means "splendor and glory." Sometimes we can get caught up in the splendor of the world and what it has to offer in the form of money, fame, big homes, automobiles, notoriety, television, being always in demand as a speaker, or other such allurements.

At such times we may be forgetting that the only thing that will overcome the giant created by such splendor and glory is God's mercy in our lives.

James 1:14 (NKJV) says, *"But each one is temped when he drawn away by his own desires and enticed."* This verse paints a picture of satan and his forces as expert fishermen!

The term "drawn away" means "to be lured like a fish is lured by bait." When you go out in a boat and throw out that great lure you have saved up to buy, it hits the water with a splash and then you troll it along behind the boat. As you reel it in, a nice big bass sees it and his own hunger entices him to take a bite at it. Then you give the line a jerk and the fish's own lust causes him to be caught and drawn away.

Satan paints a picture in your mind's eye of splendor, and his picture allures you to the point that you are enticed by your desire for what you see or dream about having. He just waits for you to bite at his lure, and then he jerks the line upward and you are drawn in by your own lust.

I have watched several artists as they've painted beautiful pictures of landscapes, mountains, and streams. As they start their paintings, they will put down a base color for background, and many times it consists of very ugly and plain colors. When you first see this, you may think to yourself, "Man, is that ugly! I wonder if he knows what he is doing."

Then, as the artist continues by putting other colors over the background, it begins to take on form and beauty.

Similarly, the pictures satan paints for you may look splendid on the surface, but behind their beauty there is always the ugliness of defeat and bondage.

Trusting in God's grace will defeat this kind of giant in your life. Allowing yourself to be overshadowed by God's mercy and love will always enable you to avoid the enemy's lures and snares in your life. Experiencing God's mercy will diminish the allure of this world's fame and power.

One of the greatest of these satanic lures in a leader's life is the desire to be a "star" who can gather all the benefits that prestige and acclaim provide even to Christian leaders.

It is always wonderful to see men and women of God who have moved into leadership within the Church of Jesus

Christ and still maintain their humility before God. I believe this comes as a result of great trials and resulting trust in the God who is always gracious.

CHAPTER 11

JONATHAN, GIANT KILLER # 5

In Second Samuel 21:20-22 (KJV) we read:

And there was yet a battle in Gath, where was a man of great stature, that had on every hand six fingers, and on every foot six toes, four and twenty in number; and he also was born to the giant. And when he defied Israel, Jonathan the son of Shimea the brother of David slew him. These four were born to the giant in Gath and fell by the hand of David, and by the hand of his servants.

Jonathan slew this gigantic man of great stature from Gath. I can remember my mother saying, "Boy, you get your fingers into everything!" Well, this fellow had six fingers on each hand and six toes on each foot! He certainly must have gotten his fingers into everything! The fact that he had so many fingers and toes suggests that he represented a bit of excess.

Being extremely busy and having your hand in every thing all at once is excessive. This "giant"—the giant of excessive time and busyness—takes down more leaders than any other through overworking, not delegating, giving more of yourself than you have to give, and literally burning out for God!

JEHOVAH HAS GIVEN

Jonathan's name means "Jehovah has given!" This is a vitally important understanding for all leaders to have; we need to know that what God has already given is enough.

We can engage in spiritual warfare by using His Spirit and His Word. Many times, though, we wear out, because we think we need to do it all by ourselves. Sometimes we take things into our own hands instead of seeking God and putting many of our problems in His hands.

We need to learn to wait upon Him for the inspiration of His Spirit, and we need to seek His wisdom. Sometimes taking a day off is the hardest thing for a man of God to do. However, leaders need time to unwind, free from the expectations of others.

The everyone-depends-on-me attitude, which is often stated as, "If I don't do it, it won't get done!" is a true killer!

I remember my first pastorate. I would put in nearly 100 hours a week in those days. I would leave for the church in the morning before my children got out of bed and I would return at night after everyone was asleep. I did that because I felt I was needed! What I didn't realize was where I was needed. I was needed at home!

But I was happy and satisfied, I thought, because I was winning the world and giving myself to my people. Then I ended up in the hospital with chest pains. The doctor said it was from anxiety and stress and that I needed to learn to take some time to rest. It was time for me to learn to delegate responsibilities and to trust others.

This "giant" of excess can sneak into your life and get you so involved that you lose and don't even know you're losing. I'm thankful for an older minister who one day took me aside and said, "Son, the only possessions you can take to Heaven with you are your children."

Hearing that, I realized what I had been missing, and I knew what he said wouldn't happen if my children didn't have a father who gives his time freely to them. This "giant" really had taken me under his control and I didn't even know it!

From then on, I started taking a day off each week to spend with my family. At first, every time the phone would ring while I was with my family I would feel guilty for not answering it. If I was playing catch with my sons and someone called, I had to fight those guilt feelings. I finally won my fight with this 12-fingered giant, and I now believe that because I did, all my children are now serving the Lord.

David had been the mentor that his men needed, and he had sown into them his wisdom of giant-killing. This caused them to become men who could face giants without him having to fight for them. They learned the skills of their leader. Their faith in God led them to victory, and it gave them the courage to face their trials with trust in God, as He led them to use the talents He had placed in their lives. The ambition of every leader should be to train and disciple competent leaders who can do all the work of the ministry, including spiritual warfare.

When I go home to be with the Father, I want to leave behind a legacy of men and women who will continue to carry on what has been left to me from my forefathers. I am a third-generation preacher. My grandfather was a Methodist preacher and a coal miner, and my father followed him as a Pentecostal preacher, evangelist, and finally a pastor. I have been preaching for 34 years, and now my son is in Bible school preparing to carry on in the ministry in the fourth generation.

I have the privilege, just like my father had before me, of planting my faith and my beliefs into my son's life. Whenever my grandsons are at my home, I lay my hands on their heads like the patriarch Jacob did with his sons. I pronounce a blessing upon them, and I ask God to call them into the ministry so they can carry on the line of ministerial anointing for a fifth generation.

Do I believe He will? Yes.

In addition, I have discipled ten others who are carrying the gospel to people in various places today. There are four others into whose lives I've been sowing seeds of ministry for the past four years. They will be carrying the gospel forth soon, and some of them have already begun.

We learn so much from the life of David. He was a true leader who was careful to reproduce his life in the lives of others. It was he who, with the help of God, formed these men—Abishai, Shibbehai, Elhanan, and Jonathan—into true giant killers! He wants to do the same in you and through you.

CHAPTER 12

A LEADER'S
BETRAYAL OF TRUST
(DESTROYING A TEAM
FROM WITHIN)

I T'S evening in Ziklag, and the night is cool. David is watching a teenage girl who is returning from the well, carrying a pitcher of water on her head.

David recognizes her, for he has known her for several years now. She is the granddaughter of his most trusted advisor, Ahithophel, who is a very wise man that has given David great counsel over the years with regard to the leadership of his men and his battle strategies.

She is Eliham's daughter. Her father has served as David's chief bodyguard, and as the captain of all his bodyguards for several years. David and Eliham have fought side by side for many years, and Eliham has always done his utmost to ensure the safety of his leader. Both Eliham and his father, Ahithophel, are really good men, for David knows they are loyal and that he can trust them.

David watches the young woman as she goes to her family's home—a happy home where Eliham lives with his children and his lovely wife. David notices that the young girl looks very much like her mother. Indeed, she is turning into a beautiful woman. David remembers some of the times when he teased her as a child and how she has always regarded him with obvious awe and admiration.

He hadn't noticed how she had grown into such a beautiful young lady until now. And he was a great judge of women, as one look at the two he had married would reveal. Before long Eliham's daughter is gone from David's view, and he imagines that it probably won't be long before she will be married. He had seen a couple of the young men hanging around her, including one of his bodyguards.

A long time has passed since that night in Ziklag. David has now become the king of all Israel. He has a fine home in Jerusalem, his capital city. It's spring again; it seems as if it came too early this year. Now is the time when kings go forth to war, and he just doesn't feel ready to do battle yet, so he decides to neglect that responsibility for a while.

Therefore, he sent Joab and the rest of Israel's fighting men to lay siege on Rabbah. After doing so, he went to the roof of his home to enjoy the cool of the evening. This was not unusual since many in that land enjoyed going to their flat roofs where they would relax in the evenings.

David now spots a young woman who is taking a bath in a pool in her garden below. His gaze locks upon her and lust begins to stir in his heart. He is so taken with the young woman's beauty that he becomes obsessed with her. He asks his servants to tell him her name, and he discovers that she is none other than Bathsheba, the daughter of the captain of his guard, Eliham. She is the young lady he had noticed before.

David had watched her grow into womanhood. Now he decides to send for her so he could have sexual relations with her. After having his way with Bathsheba, he sends her home, thinking that no one would know except for a couple of his servants.

Adulterers in Israel were subject to the death penalty. In spite of this, the king took Bathsheba who was married to one of his 30 mighty men, one of his bodyguards.

Later Bethsheba sent word to David that she was pregnant. This put the king in a real quandary. He knew that Betheshba would be stoned for adultery if this news was discovered by others. David had allowed his lack of discipline to take control of his destiny, and he had violated the trust that had existed between him and several of his team.

He sends word to Joab to give Uriah a break from the warfare and let him come home. Then David has a meal with Uriah. He tries to get him intoxicated and hopes to send him home to sleep with his wife, Bathsheba. But Uriah is a man of honor who is loyal to his comrades, so he chooses to sleep in the doorway instead. He states that it would be wrong for him to go and have and enjoyable time with his wife at home while his fellow soldiers were dying in the field.

This leads David to continue his betrayal by sending a message to Joab that commands him to put Uriah on the front lines in the battle. Soon thereafter David receives a message that Uriah has died in battle.

David then sends for Bathsheba, and he marries her in an effort to cover up their sin.

David felt that he had succeeded in keeping all these things from being exposed, and no one would ever know of their sin. Everyone was in the dark about it, except God. God told his prophet Nathan about the affair. Nathan then went to David and told him a story about someone stealing sheep. This caused David to become angry, and he declared that the thief would have to pay for his misdeed.

Then Nathan informed David that the story was about him. David repented and asked for God's forgiveness. Even though David repented, he still had to reap what he had sown. His sin would eventually lead to the death of Bathsheba's child. Also, Amnon raped his stepsister, Tamar, the daughter of Absalom. Then Absalom killed Amnon, and several years later, he overthrew David's throne and tried to kill him, and this led to his own death. Lust, when it is fulfilled, always brings destruction. Indeed, it can destroy families and even affect future generations.

Evidently, the things that happened to Bathsheba and David, along with the death of Uriah, were not kept secret. Somehow, these things were made known to those closest to Bathsheba. We don't know how long this violation of trust created an undercurrent among the leadership team, but it must have led some to feel distrustful and resentful.

From this point on we don't hear anything more about Eliham, but his father, Ahithophel, was still David's closest advisor. He must have held feelings of resentment toward David, because, when Absalom rebelled and David ran for his life, Absalom sent for Ahithophel to come to him. At this point, he turned on David and advised Absalom with regard to killing David quickly and keeping the throne.

Ahithophel knew David well as a result of working together with him and advising him in matters of war and state for many years. David was left in a very vulnerable position, because he was on the run due to his son Absalom's insurrection and plans to take his job. This all happened because David had violated the trust of his most trusted men.

The pain involved in the fall of a leader is always very deep and widespread. Frequently, when those you respect and admire fall into sin, you experience feelings of disappointment, defeat, and despair.

I remember what happened after a nationally known minister fell from grace due to adultery. Many young ministers who idolized this man's ministry left the ministry because they reasoned, "If he couldn't make it, if he failed, how can I possibly make it?" Such a loss of trust and the resulting feelings of betrayal will destroy a team.

We don't know how long Ahithophel meditated on revenge due to David's betrayal of his family. What we do know, however, is that when he found the avenue to revenge, he took it. Before the rebellion, Absalom had sent for Ahithophel in order to get his counsel against David. Two leaders who had felt wronged by their leader plotted to take over their leader's position.

This eventually cost Absalom his life, just as today this kind of unforgiveness, hurt, and bitterness could cost you the ministry God called you to do. Avoid such reactions and responses at all costs.

When Absalom refused to use all of his counsel, Ahithophel knew that David would win. Knowing this, he took his own life in order to avoid the shame the situation would cause.

Carelessness in morals is a major pitfall and snare that satan puts before God's leaders. In First Corinthians 6:9-10 (NKJV) we read: *"Do you not know that the unrighteous will not inherit the kingdom of God? Do not be deceived. Neither fornicators, nor idolaters, nor adulterers, nor homosexuals, nor sodomites, nor thieves, nor covetous, nor drunkards, nor revilers, nor extortioners will inherit the kingdom of God."* Read also Leviticus 18:22-23 and Romans 1:21-27.

Such sins are not signs of wickedness in a leader's life, but they are signs of weakness. These things happen because the leader didn't build a wall of defense around his area of weakness; therefore, in a moment of weakness, he falls.

I have seen so many good men fall through immorality. These were men I respected and looked up to. Likewise, they were men I preached for, and they preached for me. Some of these men had even trained me. They were missionaries, teachers, pastors, and friends.

Samson was called of God and anointed mightily by the Spirit, but he was driven by his lust for loose women. I have often wondered the extent of the deliverance and ministry God could have wrought through Samson if he had known how to control his lust, but it was Samson's lack of discipline in his life that led to his captivity and eventual death.

AVOID A PRIDEFUL ATTITUDE

Such a downfall can start with an attitude of pride. When one thinks, "I'm special, and God understands me and my needs" the downward spiral has been set in motion. Pride is a sin in that it is greatly despised by God. Indeed, it is the root of so many sins. It is very deceptive in that it seems to be the one sin that does not seem to carry any condemnation with it when you commit it. It deceives you and you don't recognize that you have given into it, until it's too late.

Signs of pride are manifested when you are critical of others, or you feel that no one else can do the job you do. Pride is completely self-centered and may lead you to think that things must be arranged and prioritized around you. Prideful people often find that conversations are boring unless they are focused on what they do, and they may think that others are to be used for their benefit.

AVOID THE PITFALL OF PRAYERLESSNESS

Another pitfall can come in the form of prayerlessness. Time spent with God in His presence is a prerequisite to power and leadership. If you neglect your relationship with the Father, everyone you lead will suffer. Your closeness to God will manifest itself in your lifestyle through purity and holiness. In God's presence we find direction, means, and strength.

THE PITFALL OF NEGATIVITY

Negativity is another pitfall to avoid. (See 2 Corinthians 3:18.) You can't change people by constantly being negative about them or saying negative things to them. All you will do is make them feel bad. Yes, you must stand against sin, all forms of disorder, and evil, but always be careful to balance your preaching against these things with the message of God's positive love.

A person's character is tested when he or she has various options to choose from. More power means more privileges are available to you. Remember, power is harder to control than problems, because it reveals the imperfections in our personality.

A great leader never sets himself above his followers except in carrying out his or her responsibilities. David had no one around him to whom he was accountable! We should love people and use things, not use people and love things.

In leadership, David was above everyone else, for he was the king, an absolute monarch. Almost every abuse of power comes out of someone's misunderstanding of themselves and their position.

Alexander Hamilton suggested that power could be compared to a river in that while it is kept within its boundaries, it is both beautiful and useful, but when it overflows, it brings destruction and desolation to everything and everyone in its path.

David, during his season of sin believed that his will was more important than the lives of other people. He was full of pride and lust. Corruption may come when a leader loses sight of the fact that he is given power for one purpose, and that is to serve others.

Selfish decisions always damage other people. David had closed his mind to every suggestion that he might be outside of God's will.

When Uriah told David that the men of Israel were dying and that he shouldn't live in selfish ease, David should have taken that as a rebuke or a message from God. Instead of staying at the palace, as the king, he should have been with his men. However, David's mind was set on one thing, and that was avoiding responsibility for his own secret actions.

David's first mistake in leadership was his neglect of his responsibilities as the leader of Israel.

Second Samuel 11:1 (KJV) says, *"And it came to pass, after the year was expired, at the time when kings go forth to battle, that David sent Joab, and his servants with him, and all Israel; and they destroyed the children of Ammon and besieged Rabbah. But David tarried still at Jerusalem."*

David had failed to fulfill his responsibility. It was the time when a king should have gone forth into battle. He was supposed to be with his troops, because he was their leader. If David had not been neglectful with regard to this important responsibility, he would not have been tempted on the rooftop.

The Bible says, *"For all that is in the world—the lust of the flesh, the lust of the eyes, and the pride of life—is not of the Father but is of the world"* (1 John 2:16 NKJV).

CHAPTER 13

URIAH, THE HITTITE
(DEDICATION, CONSISTENCY, AND COMRADESHIP)

THE evening was clear. The moon was full, and its light and the stars throughout the heavens seemed to fill the sky with a brilliant radiance. It was spring and Israel's army had been in battle for several weeks. They had fought and defeated the children of Ammon. Now they were encamped on the outskirts of the city of Rabbah. The siege had been going on for several days. The men had pitched their tents in the field near the city. You could see a thousand camp fires glowing across the plains.

Uriah, the Hittite, and several of his comrades were sitting around one of the camp fires, They were greatly enjoying the warmth of the fire on this cool spring evening. Everyone's spirits were high because a shipment of fresh wine and raisin cakes had arrived from Jerusalem for the soldiers. The men grew quiet as they ate the fresh cakes.

Then they broke out in laughter as Hezrai shared a joke about a Canaanite. It took Igal, the son of Nathan, awhile to figure out the punch line of the joke, but when he did, he roared with great laughter.

Everyone watched him and laughed. He was a large man, a veteran warrior that any one of them would always be willing to fight beside. The men around this fire had fought beside each other on many different occasions. As a matter of fact, they had all served as David's personal bodyguards together.

They had discussed earlier how strange it seemed to not see the big tent in the center of the camp. That was the tent that David usually occupied during battles. The tent that was in the center of camp this time held the Ark of the Covenant, and it was a great comfort for the men to know that the Ark of God was in the camp with them.

As they talked and shared, Uriah saw a lone figure in armor who was heading toward their camp fire. As he drew closer, they realized it was General Joab. He walked straight toward them. They rose to their feet and stood in front of him. He faced Uriah and asked him to accompany him back to his tent.

Uriah did so, and, upon arriving at Joab's tent, he was informed that he was being sent back to Jerusalem to give King David a report on how the war was progressing. He was to leave first thing in the morning, and a horse would be provided for him.

The next day Uriah left at dawn and headed for Jerusalem. It was about a 30-mile trip. He arrived at the king's palace late in the evening, and one of David's servants recognized him at the door. Uriah had been here many times while he served on guard duty.

After a short wait, the servant took him into the presence of King David who demanded that he tell him how Joab and the other soldiers were and how the battle was going.

Then David told him to go home and wash up. Uriah had no idea that there might be an ulterior motive behind his king's commands. The king had meat prepared for him to eat, but Uriah slept at the door of David's house with the servants and refused to go home.

One of the servants came to David the next morning and told him that Uriah had slept at his door instead of returning home to his wife. David then called for Uriah and asked him why he didn't go home after having been gone for so long and having just returned from a long journey.

Then Uriah showed what kind of attitudes governed his life. He said, *"The ark, and Israel, and Judah, abide in tents; and my lord Joab, and the servants of my lord, are encamped in the open fields; shall I then go into mine house, to eat and to drink, and to lie with my wife? as thou livest, and as thy soul liveth, I will not do this thing"* (2 Sam. 11:11 KJV).

This man clearly had an ethical standard that he abided by. He would not enjoy a life of ease while his friends and comrades were facing hardships. His attitude was, "I won't let someone else carry my responsibility."

In fact, he was so loyal to the cause and to his comrades that he could not even consider taking any kind of personal advantage of the situation. His heart and soul were on the field with his friends who were fighting and dying. His heart was where the Ark of God was. Uriah was willing to carry his load, and this must have made it hard for David to deceive him.

Uriah was a man who had high moral standards for his life and his work. He would never compromise those standards.

We rarely see such loyalty to others and their cause.

As leaders, when we are choosing our "mighty men," we must take a good look at their standards of life. In Uriah we see a man who was the same at home, work, or play. It is always a comfort to know upon what convictions your team members will take their stand. Uriah was a man who would always stand beside his leader and care about his welfare.

Whenever an accusation is brought against this kind of man, you must stand by him as a leader and say, "I'm sorry, but I can't believe that report, because I know the life of this man and the standards he has set for himself."

With this type of team member, if you need help or assistance, all you have to do is ask. He is a faithful comrade who is willing to sacrifice his time and strength in behalf of your cause. In his selfishness David didn't realize or even want to see the caliber of the man he had before him.

Next, David tried another approach to get Uriah to go home to his wife, but this man was firm in his faith and he was not about to be dissuaded. David told Uriah to stay for the rest of the day and not leave until the next day. That night David invited him to his home for supper. He did his best to get Uriah drunk, figuring that if he was intoxicated, he wouldn't know what he was doing and would then head home to his wife.

Yet, even after being seduced by drink, he went to the servants' quarters to sleep and still refused to go home. Now David figured his only choice would be to send a command to Joab to have Uriah placed in the forefront of battle in the hopes that he would get killed. Uriah was a very loyal servant and he had to carry the letter to Joab, not knowing that he was carrying his own death sentence.

David's selfish attitude at this point tells us that some leaders will use or manipulate those who are most loyal to them for their own personal advancement, advantage, or security. Uriah was about to take the fall for David's secret sins.

Uriah may not have killed 800 in battle or killed a lion in a pit, but the kinds of attitudes and standards he exhibited in his life made him one of David's most valuable mighty men.

Even though his name was last on the list of David's mighty warriors, his attitudes could have made him one of the first. His was not a flashy life that was filled with the fame of battles, but he was a steady, faithful worker, who remained loyal to the Ark (Jesus), to his leader, and to all his comrades. Uriah was a man you could depend on to fight by your side and not betray your trust when he was absent from the battlefield.

I have personally known one such team player for over 25 years now. He grew up in a home with strict standards during the '50s and early '60s. You know him by his disciplines; and, as a comrade, he is invaluable. For example, I know that he will faithfully mow and manicure the church lawn as is needed and prepare the altar for communion each first Sunday of the month.

Twenty-five years ago he took on the responsibility for children's church, as well, because no one else would do it. Today he still teaches children's church. He goes out every weekend and mows the lawns of the elderly. When I was recovering from surgery, he would come to my house and mow the lawn. He also built rock gardens and improved all the landscaping around our home.

This kind soul always asks what he can do for me and my family. Last year, when another brother in the church had heart surgery, this team player went to the man's home daily, trying to improve his situation in whatever ways he could.

Also, every Sunday he shares Christ at a nearby juvenile detention center.

When we need to have flyers handed out or evangelism done, he is always available. I remember one time when we were circulating some printed flyers about our church in the community. This man went door to door, reaching out to hundreds of homes. Then he would come back and see if anyone had any flyers left over so he could distribute some more. He visited 1,500 homes by himself!

If anyone is in need, this modern day Uriah is ready to stand with them in any way he can to help them in their time of difficulty. His faithfulness and humility as an elder of the church are truly unmatchable. For example, when there is a prayer meeting, you can always count on the fact that he will remain in intercessory prayer at the altar after everyone else has gone home.

He is truly consistent, and the word "consistency" is defined as "agreement with previous acts, statements, or decisions, not contradictory, a single set of principles."

Our leaders need to have consistency in their words and in every aspect of their lives. We should expect consistency, not excuses, from our leaders. The enemies of consistent Christian living are laziness, greed, prestige, self-righteousness, pleasures of the flesh, and busyness. To be consistent requires you to have a standard of living such as that demonstrated by the life of Uriah.

I remember speaking to one of our pastors who pastored a large church that had openings for an assistant pastor and a children's church pastor. At this time he had about ten pastors on staff. I remember that he had a dinner for his church ministers at which he announced these two openings.

He asked if there were any volunteers for the position of children's church pastor. It seemed that no one was interested in such a "lowly position." As a result, the pastor left the assistant pastor's position vacant and later went outside the church and hired an assistant.

After some time had passed, he shared with me that the man who would be humble enough to take the children's church position would have become his new assistant pastor, but since no one was willing to take the lower position, he had felt he had to search outside the congregation for the one who would become his assistant pastor.

Unfortuantely, there were no Uriahs on his staff.

CHAPTER 14

ONE LEADER CONSPICUOUSLY MISSING

(DISOBEDIENCE, DECEPTION, AND SELF-SEEKING)

AS I read through the list of David's mighty men in Second Samuel 23, I was surprised to find that one name was missing. It was the name of a man who probably did more to bring honor and greatness to David than any other warrior. Through his great abilities he won more decisive battles for David than anyone else ever did.

In addition, he did more to expand the kingdom than anyone else had done. The only one who deserved more glory than this warrior was David himself. Even so, he is conspicuously absent from the list.

As I read the biblical accounts about this leader, I began to realize why David did not allow this man to get into his "hall of fame." While David used this man's extraordinary abilities as a leader, he simply did not trust him. The reason for the king's lack of trust was that he knew this man could be devious and even rebellious.

Even though he seemed to be a loyal and loving subject or team member, it appears that he would have taken David's job if the opportunity to do so had presented itself. Nonetheless, he became a man of great reputation who would do anything, including murder, to protect his position. Whether his actions came from the motive to protect David or to achieve his own selfish purposes could be debated. However, it appears that David could tell what his motives were. This man was one of David's nephews, a son of his older sister, and he was most likely very close in age to David.

This man's brother made the list of David's mighty men, even though he had accomplished less than his brother.

Ultimately, David had his son, Solomon, execute this man soon after he turned the kingdom over to Solomon. Perhaps he did this to protect Solomon and his throne. David was concerned about him because this man had advocated for David's other son, Adonijah, to be the next king. David chose Solomon, however, to be his successor.

The man I'm referring to was Joab, who was known as the Prince of the Armies of Israel. He was David's commanding general and adviser, and his military victories had greatly strengthened David's monarchy.

One of Joab's adversaries was Saul's commanding general, Abner. Abner had been responsible for Joab's younger brother's death, even though Abner had tried to avoid it. He had been pushed to a point where he had no choice.

Abner had convinced Joab to end the fighting of Israelites against Israelites. He then convinced Israel to follow David, made peace with David, and offered to consolidate Israel under David.

When Joab heard the news and realized that he might have a competitor, the man he knew to be responsible for his brother's death in battle, he began to develop plans for Abner's death. David had no knowledge of what was transpiring.

When Abner arrived on the scene, Joab took him aside in the gate to speak with him privately. He seemingly reached out to Abner in friendship, then grabbed him and stabbed him to death with his sword.

When David heard about Abner's murder he grew very angry, so angry that he cursed Joab and his house, because he felt that Joab had murdered an honorable man.

At Abner's funeral, David declared his feelings about Joab before all Israel. This is recorded in Second Samuel 3:38-39 (NKJV): *"Do you not know that a prince and a great man has fallen this day in Israel? And I am weak today, though anointed king; and these men, the sons of Zeruiah, are too harsh for me. The Lord shall repay the evildoer according to his wickedness."*

In all likelihood, this was the point at which Joab had crossed the line in his relationship with his leader, for David no longer trusted Joab. At one point in their relationship, David had lost faith in Joab as a leader and had appointed Amasia to replace Joab as general over all the armies of Israel, soon after the death of Absalom.

Joab found the opportunity to greet Amasia as they were pursuing Sheba according to David's orders and took Amasia by the beard to kiss him, then plunged his sword into his stomach!

From these two instances we see that Joab was insecure and would attack anyone who might be able to replace him in his position. He would stop at nothing, including murder, to realize his goals.

When David had exiled Absalom for the murder of his stepbrother, Joab had taken it upon himself to deceive David into bringing Absalom back to Jerusalem. The Bible tells us that Joab had perceived that the king's heart was toward Absalom. This was what Joab himself thought he had perceived, but he never asked David about it. He just set out to trick David into bringing Absalom home.

He did this by searching for and finding a wise woman. He told her how to go before the king and request help for her son. When she did so, David promised to help her.

Then she explained that it was his son (Absalom) that she was referring to, and said, "You have now sworn that you would do it."

David asked, "Was it Joab who put you up to this?"

She told him that it was Joab's plan.

Because he had sworn this, David had to allow Absalom to return to Jersualem. Later Absalom plotted to overthrow his father and usurp his throne.

This was another deception to add to Joab's list of failings as a leader. Obviously, he was not much of a team player. He went behind the back of his leader and did what he felt would be best. Certainly he was ambitious, but he was not trustworthy, even though sometimes he may have been well-intentioned.

When Absalom had his father on the run for his life, he sent his army after his father with orders to kill him. When David's army was getting ready to leave and do battle with Absalom's, on the other hand, he charged his men not to kill his son. During the battle, Absalom, who had long, flowing hair, got his hair caught in a tree limb and was left hanging there by the hairs of his head.

This fact was reported to Joab, who went to see for himself. The men reminded Joab of David's command not to harm his son, but Joab disobeyed this command and killed Absalom.

Here we see a member of David's leadership team making a decision which was completely contrary to the directives given by the leader. He did so, perhaps, based on the assumption that he knew what was best for his boss, even though it meant absolute disobedience against the wishes of the man in charge.

I once had a board member who was similar to Joab. This man would sit quietly in the boardroom and listen to me and the others talking. If he disagreed, he never stated his thoughts; instead, he seemingly just went along with the rest of us.

Later, we discovered that when he disagreed with us he would not express his opinion. Instead, he would go to other church members who were not members of the board and sow seeds of discord by letting them in on his points of disagreement. He would make innuendos by saying such things as, "You would not believe what goes on in those board meetings behind closed doors."

We found this out as members began to ask us what we were doing in the board meetings that was "so bad." Of course, we did nothing but conduct church business and develop plans for the church, but this brother was using his position to find ways to sow distrust toward all of the leadership except himself. Through his undermining of authority and sowing of discord, he was dividing "the camp" for his own motives. We clearly had a "Joab" in our leadership.

LETTING GO OF OUR "TEDDY BEARS"

Insecurity can cause great turmoil in the heart of a leader. Recently on a Sunday morning during the offering, a child walked up front to put her offering in the coin jar. She was really having a hard time doing so, because she was trying to put the coins in the bottle and hold her teddy bear at the same time. Her bear was almost as big as she was. I can hardly remember seeing her in church without her teddy bear. It seemed that Teddy was currently her security, but, in this case, Teddy was keeping her from giving to God!

We can use many things to cover our insecurities when we are little, but when we grow up and still cling to something that keeps us from being able to freely give ourselves to God and trust Him, we will find ourselves in turmoil.

Everyone is familiar with anxiety and worry. They are some of the most counter- productive things we can ever engage in. As someone said, worry is like a rocking chair; it gives you something to do, but it won't take you anywhere.

Becoming distressed over uncertainties constitutes real or imagined threats to our well-being. Joab's insecurities were rooted in his fear that others wanted his job. Like him, we may feel vulnerable and inadequately protected against real or perceived threats. Such things as the fear of social rejection can easily create real feelings of insecurity in our hearts. Whether they are real or imagined threats doesn't matter, because they cause much anxiety in either case.

To overcome this kind of problem we need to let go of our "teddy bears"—those things we cling to for a sense of security. After open-heart surgery, I was given a teddy bear that was named "Sir Cough-A-Lot."

I needed that bear in order to walk, and he would help me as I hugged him to my chest. If I needed to cough or sneeze,

I would simply squeeze teddy to my chest and this would help alleviate some of the pain.

I remember people staring at me when I would walk into a store or a restaurant with my teddy bear in my hands. I'm sure the sight of a 54-year-old man carrying a teddy bear was very strange! But finally the day came when I was able to put the teddy bear up on the shelf with a thank you, hopefully never to pick him up again. He was no longer needed.

Many times we don't face the truth about our insecurities concerning being in leadership. This comes from a lack of trust in God or a lack of experience. Romans 8:31 (NKJV) says: *"What then shall we say to these things? If God be for us, who can be against us?"*

When you feel isolated, the truth of God may be found in Psalms 23:4 (KJV): *"Yea, though I walk through the valley of the shadow of death, I will fear no evil: for thou art with me; thy rod and they staff they comfort me."*

Keep feeding on the Word of God and committing yourself to Him. Doing so will require you to grow in your knowledge of Him and His love. Realize that peace of mind does not depend on solving all the problems you face and being perfect all the time. Remember, anxiety will not get rid of tomorrow's problems.

As we look at these instances from the stories of the lives of David's men, we can readily see why Joab was not included in the Bible's list of David's mighty warriors.

While Joab was a leader of men and a wise military man, he manipulated, deceived, disobeyed, and tried to force his will over that of his team leader. As a result, he was never able to fulfill his destiny.

Yes, he was heroic, but the motives for his heroism always seemed to center on seeking power and position for his own glory! When you have someone like this on your team, you need to say to him or her what we often hear on a very popular television show: "You're fired!"

CHAPTER 15

STAYING OUT OF THE "JOAB MENTALITY"

(UNDERSTANDING YOUR AUTHORITY)

THE church service is in full swing, and the worship is awesome, because the people have entered into the very Presence of God. This is a true revival, and the evangelist has hit the pulpit at "full steam."

You can see small beads of sweat on his brow as he paces back and forth under the anointing. He is expounding from Matthew 3:11 (NKJV): *"I indeed baptize you with water unto repentance, but He who is coming after me is mightier than I, whose sandals I am not worthy to carry. He will baptize you with the Holy Spirit and fire."*

In this verse John the Baptist is speaking about Jesus and how John recognized the dignity and preeminence of Christ above himself. John was telling the people that he could baptize them in water, but that's all he could do. This was true even though John had much power, for he came in the spirit and power of Elias. But Christ has far more power and authority. John truly was great, but Christ made him seem small by comparison.

As I read the words Jesus spoke about the humility of John, I realize it is a great comfort to every faithful minister to think that Jesus Christ is mightier than he or she is. The Lord Jesus Christ can do that which they cannot do. His strength is perfected in our weakness.

I wonder what it would be like to serve a savior who could not do more than we can do for ourselves. It is a great consolation for us to know that He is *"...able to do exceedingly abundantly above all that we ask or think, according to the power which works in us"* (Eph. 3:20 NKJV).

Why would anyone serve a God who wasn't able to do the impossible for them? When I was 14 years old, I fell from a jungle gym on the school playground. I was hanging upside down and eventually fell hard on my neck. The fall crushed three vertebrae in my spine, I was put in the hospital for a week. The doctors required me to lie in a special position on my back. Then they placed a body cast on me from my neck to my thighs.

Around that time my pastor came by for a visit, and he laid his hands on me and prayed, asking God to heal my spine. Since I was already in the cast, there was no way to know if I was healed at that time. Then, one month after I was discharged, I had to return to the hospital in order to replace the body cast with a lighter one. At that point, when they X-rayed my back, the vertebrae were completely restored and I was sent home for good! I am really glad we serve a God who is able to do the impossible!

Then, as the evangelist continued to speak, the Spirit of the Lord began to lead me in another direction with regard to the speaker's text. I asked myself, "What was John saying to those around him that day?" I began to search through my Bible, looking excitedly for various passages that were coming to my mind. I didn't mean to, but I must have made a lot of noise as I riffled through the Bible, flapping pages in a hurried fashion.

THE AUTHORITY OF THE FEET

I discovered that there are 21 references to shoes in the Bible. Now, as you know, shoes protect the feet. As I thought more about this, I began to realize that the enemies of Christ are placed beneath His feet. Under His feet! Then I thought of Joshua and how God had promised that his territory would be wherever his feet would tread.

When Joshua was fighting in Gibeon (see Josh. 10), his army was fighting against the armies of five kings. These five were the kings of Jerusalem, Hebron, Jarmuth, Lachish, and Eglon.

God helped Joshua and his men by sending large hailstones out of Heaven which killed many of the men who were serving under the five kings. The rest were being destroyed by Israel.

Then Joshua prayed and the sun stood still. These five kings turned in fear and ran to Makkedah, where they hid in a cave. Some of Joshua's men saw them go into the cave and sent word to back to him, and Joshua told them to roll huge boulders in front of the cave entrance and close the five kings inside.

When the battle was finished, Joshua and his men returned to Makkedah and brought out the five kings. He then told his captains to place their feet upon the necks of the five kings. Joshua wanted his men to understand how it felt to have your enemies under their authority.

God says: *"Sit thou at my right hand, until I make thine enemies thy footstool"* (Ps. 110:1 KJV).

What, then, do shoes have to do with what Jesus said in Matthew 3? A shoe was a symbol of the power or authority of a man. It represented a man's authority over his domain. He could own the land he walked upon, because planting his foot on something usually was a symbol of lordship or ownership.

When one loosed his shoe and handed it to another, he was abdicating and transferring his right and title to a given property.

We see a good example of this custom in Ruth 4:7 (NKJV): *"Now this was the custom in former times in Israel concerning the redeeming and exchanging, to confirm anything: one man took off his sandal and gave it to the other, and this was a confirmation in Israel."*

In Ruth 3:4 we see Ruth going to the threshing floor of Boaz, as Naomi had directed her to do. She was to wait there until he had fallen asleep, then she was to slip down to the threshing floor and uncover his feet and lie down at his feet. When Boaz woke up, he was surprised to find Ruth lying at his uncovered feet.

The Bible says that he was startled awake at midnight and found a woman lying at his feet. He asked her who she was and she told him that she was Ruth. Then she asked him to "take her under his wing," because he was her near kinsman. By doing these things Ruth had placed herself under his authority.

Basically, she had proposed marriage to him at his feet. He agreed to do as she had requested and told her to sleep through the rest of the night and leave early in the morning before anyone woke and found a woman at the threshing floor.

According to the Word of God, when a kinsman refused to perform his duty to the family of his deceased relative, his widow was directed to pull off his shoe and spit in his face to show distain. Then his house would become known as "the house of the shoeless man." This was not the case with Boaz, for he was willing to do his duty.

What we see in these verses is that shoes represent the authority of a person. When Moses came into the Presence of God at the burning bush, God said to him, "Take off your shoes, because the ground you stand on is holy." (See Exodus 3:5.)

When Joshua came into the presence of the Angel of the Lord at Jericho, he was told to take off his shoes, because he was on holy ground. Why?

Because man's authority cannot stand in the Presence of God's authority. Man's authority and man's power are completely inadequate in the Presence of God!

John the Baptist was not worthy to carry the shoes of the Messiah of the world. Jesus was the Son of God. He was full of the Holy Ghost. The most John could hope for was a portion of the Spirit. Jesus was empowered with the full rights of Sonship. John could only desire to be a friend of the Bridegroom. He was an Old Testament believer, and he had a call to prepare the way for Jesus to usher in the Kingdom of God. The Bible tells us that the gospel of the Kingdom of God has been preached ever since John's ministry.

John could not have the same authority Jesus had, and he could not even carry the shoes of such a Man of authority. He could not walk where Christ would walk, do what Christ would do, or be empowered like Christ was empowered. Christ had come in the full authority of the Spirit!

Jesus had come to set the captives free, open the eyes of the blind, cast out the demons that oppressed people, raise the dead, heal the leper and the lame, preach the kingdom, and bring salvation to the lost. John, on the other hand, had come to preach repentance and to baptize those who did repent.

Most parents have watched their children try on their shoes. I remember one time when my 3-year-old grandson tried to put his feet into my size-11 cowboy boots. My boots covered his legs up to his hips, and when he would try to walk in them, he would fall. He simply could not fill my shoes.

Similarly, Jesus' shoes were, in a very real sense, too big for John to fill! No man before Christ could carry the kind of spiritual authority that Jesus carried.

Jesus put on His sandals and walked about Israel. As He did so, He healed people, cast out devils, raised the dead, restored the paralyzed, opened deaf ears, gave sight to blind eyes, gave the gift of speech to those who were mute, multiplied the bread and fish, and stopped the storm.

Then, as He walked to the cross in order to take away our sins, He took authority away from all principalities and powers and placed them under His feet. (This was His authority in action.)

His authority was for those who were poor, the ones who had been utterly rejected and could not pay their own bills. It was for the broken-hearted folk, as well, and for all those who are bruised and oppressed. His authority provided for the total healing of the person—physical, emotional, and spiritual. He set the captives free, prisoners who had been held against their wills behind bars and in lowly dungeons throughout their lives. Likewise, He brought freedom to those who were captive to their emotions and the will of others.

He still does this today by bringing liberty to those who are captive to drugs, alcohol, attention-getting, fears, hurts, and all manner of sins! He brings light to those who are in darkness, where even a little light could hurt their eyes.

Jesus has come to open the eyes of the spiritually blind, those who have been blinded by the world and satan. He does this so they will see the truth of God's good news. Yes, He came to set at liberty those who are bruised, crushed, and broken down by calamity. As you can see, the sandals of Jesus were shoes that were way too big for John to wear or even to carry.

In John 1:12 (NKJV) we read these words: *"But as many as received Him [Jesus], to them gave He the right [authority] to become children of God, to those who believe in His name."*

In Mark 16:17 (KJV) Jesus said, *"And these signs shall follow them that believe; In my name shall they cast out devils; they shall speak with new tongues; they shall take up serpents; and if they drink any deadly thing, it shall not hurt them; they shall lay hands on the sick, and they shall recover."* That is true spiritual authority!

What did our "Near Kinsman" do for us? He handed over the shoes to His "next of kin" (His church) and said, "Here is My authority." You see, Jesus has given His shoes to His church—to all those who believe in Him.

THE PRODIGAL SON

In the story of the Prodigal Son we see a young man who demanded his share of the inheritance from his father early. He wanted to leave home and live the life that he had dreamed that money could give to him. He took his inheritance and lived a wild life. When his money ran out, so did all of his friends. The only job he could get was as a farmhand, working in the pigpen. In other words, he had to "slop the hogs."

Eventually he became so hungry that he had to eat with the pigs. When he came to himself, he remembered that even the servants in his father's house had it better than he did. He reasoned, "At least they have food, a roof over their heads, and clean clothes to wear."

He then decided to return to his father and ask him if he could be a servant in his father's house. His father saw him coming down the lane, and he ran to greet his son. He gave him a big hug, then turned to a servant and said, "My son who was gone has returned home. Bring me a robe."

The father placed a robe on his son, put a ring on his finger, and gave him new shoes to wear. Each of these items serves as a symbol of position and authority in his father's house. The Prodigal Son was now able to wear the robe of a ruler, the signet ring of the family, and brand new shoes.

ON WHAT IS YOUR AUTHORITY BASED?

On what do you base your authority? The apostle Paul said in Ephesians 6:15: *"Having your feet shod with the preparation of the gospel of peace."*

Why are our feet so important in all of this? It's because that is where our authority lies in a figurative sense; our feet are symbolic of the authority we have in Christ.

True spiritual authority is based on what God has given to us in His Word.

In Ephesians 6, Paul is speaking of spiritual armor when he shares about having our feet shod with the preparation of the gospel of peace. Military shoes in Paul's day were used to defend and protect the soldier's feet from the traps that had been put down by the enemy, which might be in the form of hidden sharp sticks and other snares. Those who fell upon the sharp sticks obviously became unfit to march and fight and many actually died.

When Peter was arrested and was facing death, an angel came to free him from his bondage. In Acts 12:5-11, we see that the first thing that happened was that the angel brought light with him. Light filled the cell where Peter was sleeping. It's interesting to note that the angel actually had to shake Peter to wake him up.

Sometimes we actually get comfortable in our bondage. Even though there was light in the cell, Peter still did not see clearly. He thought he was dreaming. His mind still did not see the truth. An angel was waiting to take him to freedom, and Peter didn't believe that what he was seeing was real. When the angel woke him up, the chains fell off his hands and legs. Peter was now free from the shackles, but he was still in prison. In order to get truly free, he had to put on clothing similar to that of the Prodigal Son.

People can be saved and set free and still remain in bondage in some areas of their lives. They need authority to truly break free. The angel told Peter to gird himself and put on his sandals. Next, the angel told Peter to put on his robe and follow him.

In this example God is showing us the way to freedom, which requires us to put on the garments of salvation and prepare our feet for walking with the gospel wherever we go.

Why do we have so many problems concerning living and operating in authority? What prevents men like Joab from moving in true authority? What has stopped the flow of spiritual power and authority in ministry today? The answer can be most simply and directly stated as *dirty feet*!

When you understand this statement and grasp how feet are a symbolic representation of walking in authority, then you realize the meaning of some of Jesus' statements to His disciples. One of these is found in Matthew 10:14, Mark 6:11, Luke 9:5, and Luke 10:11 (four different versions of the same command). *"And whosoever shall not receive you, nor hear you, when ye depart thence, out of the house or city, shake off the dust under your feet..."* (Mark 6:11 KJV).

In our daily lives, even when counseling others, we can find ourselves in sin through wrong thinking, lust, anger, rejection, hardness of heart, etc. Any of these wrong thoughts, feelings, and responses will quickly contaminate our spiritual power and authority and our ability to move in God's ways.

This can lead to attitudes similar to those of Joab. We can become disobedient and use deception and manipulation to substitute for the lack of true authority in our lives.

When you are moving under your own strength and power, disobedience and deception will come easy. Before you know it, you will become burned out spiritually and physically, and you will turn to other means to hold on to your place of leadership.

Many times these attitudes are born out of fear and insecurity which will cause you to distrust the motives of those who are trying to assist you. You will feel threatened and fear that you will be replaced.

When these things happen, you need to take time to get refreshed and stand back and look at your own motives and situation from a new perspective. It's hard to see the truth from a burned-out perspective. You need to spend time alone with God.

I remember coming to such a place in my own ministry. It seemed as if I had hit a wall with full force. I realized I could not carry on in the state of mind I was experiencing. I called all the church elders together and told them what I was experiencing. Then I asked them for two months off from my responsibilities in order to find restoration for myself.

During that time I would attend the church and allow them to help me in my efforts to find restoration both emotionally and spiritually. This, along with time alone seeking God and reading His Word, helped me to view my situation from a spiritual perspective and step away from the burn-out I had been experiencing. I had to come to a place where I realized that I hadn't dealt properly with some wounds and hurts I had received through ministry. Once this was accomplished, I was ready to step back into my leadership role.

Ministry requires clean feet! The priests of the Tabernacle always went to the laver to wash their feet before ministering in the things of the Lord. At the Last Supper Jesus girded himself with a towel and began to kneel before each of the disciples to wash their feet. One by one, He would place their feet into the basin of water and wash off the dust and dirt from their daily walk. When he came to Peter, the disciple asked, "Lord, why are you washing my feet?"

Jesus answered, "What I am doing you do not understand now, but you will know after this."

Peter said, "You shall never wash my feet." Peter was refusing his Lord's ministry to him. Perhaps this was because he felt that Jesus was too good to be in that position. Having Jesus wash his feet was too humbling of an experience for Peter to accept.

Jesus responded, "If I do not wash you, you have no part in Me."

Peter then said, "Lord, not my feet only, but also my hands and my head!" He was ready now, for he knew he wanted to have a part in Christ.

Notice Jesus' response, "He who has bathed needs only to wash his feet, but is completely clean; and you are clean, but not all of you." In effect, he was saying, "No, you don't have to get saved again. No, you have already been washed clean. Only part of you gets contaminated by contact with the world. It's your feet, Peter!"

The believer is cleansed from his sins once and for all. But he needs to come before God during this earthly life to get his daily sins washed clean through foot washing.

We have to deal with sins such as anger when someone insults us or does something against us or hurts us. To say you will never get hurt in ministry would be to live in a fairy tale. There are times when you are just getting ready to walk up to the pulpit and conduct services and just then someone stops you in the hall or vestibule and says, "Pastor, I have a conflict with you and want to talk to you about it." Or it may come in this classic form: "Pastor, you know I love you, but...!"

There are issues we must deal with that may arouse lust, unforgiveness, anger, and even bitterness. Jesus told His disciples to get the dust off their feet. One reason He told them to do so may be found in the rejection they received in the homes or cities they visited. If we carry those rejections within our hearts, we will have dust on our feet or we will have dirtied our authority. In those cases we will have dirty feet and will need to go to Christ for a foot washing. Foot washing is about those daily sins that accumulate in our lives, and we need others to help us get free from them.

If Joab had only been able to make himself accountable to others. What happens when we get contaminated by this world's attitudes? We easily grow lax toward other sins or we become apathetic with regard to our service to God.

I remember being called to preach at a church several years ago. I had never been there before and had never met the pastor or any members of the congregation. Another minister I knew was conducting a meeting there and had requested that the pastor let him use several speakers during the week. It was at his request that I was called, and I was asked to come and speak.

That morning, around 3 A.M., I was awakened by the Holy Spirit. He spoke just two words to me: *"Bal Peor!"* I got up and wrote down the Scripture and prayed for a while about what God wanted from me. I was led to prepare a message on the sins of Bal Peor, the place where Israel sinned against the Lord by lusting after the women of Moab and were led into sin.

At this point I began to get a little nervous about that night's service. God was asking me to speak on sexual sins in the midst of that congregation! The truth is I would have never spoken on this subject, unless the Lord had clearly told me to do so. However, I could not deny His will.

That night I got up and read my text and proceeded to speak on secret sexual sins, such as pornography and people having affairs in the church with other believers. As I spoke, I saw the pastor's jaw drop. Anger and surprise crossed his face.

Nonetheless, I braced myself and continued. In my mind I was silently praying, "God, you got me into this, so help me out!" I proceeded to the altar call by asking everyone to bow their heads. I asked for those to whom God was speaking about their sexual sins to stand up and come forward to the altar and get right with God.

To my amazement, over 60 percent of the church responded! Following the service, the pastor came to me and said, "Thank you for obeying the Lord; I did not know what was happening."

BE CLEAN!

When we allow so many things from worldly defilement to accumulate on our "shoes of authority," we can become complacent and apathetic and caught up in our own desires and survival.

When this happens, we become like Joab who was concerned about himself and his fears. Isaiah 52:11 (KJV) says, *"Be ye clean, that bear the vessels of the Lord."*

CHAPTER 16

MOVING INTO POSITION

MANY years ago in a place called Shushan there lived a beautiful young woman. She was single and lived with her uncle because her parents had died. One day she was doing her daily chores when a man with a group of soldiers arrived at her home. They informed her that she had been chosen to participate in a contest. The king had declared that young women were to be gathered from everywhere and brought to the palace, for he was searching for a new queen. This beautiful young woman was Esther, and she was taken to the palace with other young women.

How could this young woman become a person of great authority and have the power to affect the lives of many for generations to come? As you continue reading, you will discover the answer to this question.

In the '90s I scheduled a young man, Pastor Nathan Bird of the Worship Center, in St. Albans, New York, to teach our annual Leadership Conference. Brother Bird taught on the subject of moving in authority. Over the years I have incorporated some of his teaching into mine. Therefore, the teaching on moving into authority that I share in this chapter has been influenced by the knowledge he shared with us.

Without doubt, the church needs to be directed. Persons in the pew need to be specifically directed into the will of God. They are not to be given suggestions and they are not to be advised, but they need to be *directed*. One of the means of finding God's direction for the church is to move into proper authority.

I looked through the Old Testament and didn't find the word "authority" used more than twice. Both times it appeared in the Book of Esther. This is the only book in the Old Testament that translates the Hebrew term for "authority" into English.

Let's start with Esther 9:29. Then we will define "authority" and see how Esther moved into the place of authority. This will teach us a great deal about our own attitudes and how to move properly in the use of spiritual authority.

Esther 9:29 (NKJV): *"Then Queen Esther, the daughter of Abihail, with Mordecai the Jew, wrote with full authority to confirm this second letter."* Now, Esther and Mordecai were given authority to write this decree and have it stamped by the king and have it distributed throughout all the provinces of the Jews. They did this with the king's full authority. This authority established two holidays for them that would be celebrated throughout all of the provinces of the Jews and are still observed today as feast days.

Now, to understand true authority, we need to see how Esther got to the place of authority. As you will see, a certain process was involved.

Many think that authority simply comes with appointment to a particular position. Certainly a degree of influence will come that way, but true authority is actually delegated to us by God, and He has a process that will prepare a leader to move into authority.

A lack of understanding of true authority will often lead to a misuse of authority such as we see in the life of Joab.

Now, to do justice to our explanation of "authority," we need to at least examine it from its dictionary denotation. The word "authority" stems from the word "author." An author is someone who creates or originates. That's why we call Jesus the Author and Finisher of our faith! In Him authority was established, created, and exhibited, so we look to Him as the One who has actually made this happen. He is the Author of authority!

Authority basically establishes for us in several areas of power: the power to command, the power to determine, the power to influence, and the power to judge.

An authority is one who is accepted as a credible and reliable source of information. Many courts call upon authorities or expert witnesses, because they are the accepted sources of information that are considered unquestionable and absolute.

In the church world some may consider such authority to be like a dictatorship—too much control. People who feel this way might say, "Hey, you can't have total control, and you can't function as an absolute leader in this body. There are other people who have a voice, who have reason, who have capability, and who have ability." These people may question and challenge authority.

Why does this happen? It's because so many have abused their power and authority. This leads some to say, "Hold on, we're not going to allow that anymore."

Are these challengers just in their reaction? Many times they are, but, over all. I would say that such a mentality was given to our society during the '60s, when many rebelled and questioned all authority, even God's.

There are those who will always question authority. They look for things to demean those who are in authority or try to find a way to make them fall. First, they try to destroy the credibility of the one who is in authority or try to reveal his or her weaknesses, sinfulness, or untrustworthiness. Then they attack the authority figure's motives.

This is what happened to Moses, when one of the elders, Korah, came to him and said, "Who made you any better than the rest of us?"

We see this same attitude today, as well. For example, someone might say to one who is in authority, "All of the body is holy, not just you. Why should you be leading us?"

I wonder if this is where the doctrine of universalism was first established. I can remember a time when a deacon came to me and stated, "All the body is anointed—every single believer. Who made you boss?"

My answer was a straightforward one: "God did!"

You see, human eyes see only man, and they do not recognize the fact that true spiritual authority comes from God.

The Bible tells us that God gave gifts unto men. (See Ephesians 4:8.) Paul outlines those ministry gifts for us: apostles, prophets, evangelists, pastors, and teachers. (See 1 Corinthians 12:28.) The Greek word that is translated as "gifts" here is not "charisma" which is used with regard to the gifts of the Holy Spirit. Rather, it is a word that means "character."

God gave the men who serve in ministry gifts the character or personality to be leaders. He anoints them to become these leaders. His anointing gives them the character of an apostle, a prophet, an evangelist, a pastor, or a teacher. God gives His leaders the gifts they need to lead in their individual capacities. These special gifts are not given to the entire body of believers.

EXPERTS IN THE WORD OF GOD

Now there is another reason why our authority has been diminished: we have not functioned as experts. To be an authority in the Body of Christ we need to be experts in the Word of God.

When this is not the case, a local church becomes powerless and without influence in its community. Why? Because the leadership has to submit to the fellowship. This is a violation of God's divine order. That's why First Samuel 15:24 (NKJV) has to stay in our spirits: *"Then Saul said to Samuel, 'I have sinned, for I have transgressed the commandment of the Lord and your words, because I feared the people and obeyed their voice...."* Saul was rejected as king because he feared the people and listened to their voice instead of fulfilling and hearkening to God's commands.

The word "hearkened" is used twice in the Book of Genesis. It is used to represent Adam hearkening to his wife, Eve, and Abram harkening to his wife, Sara. Both of these men failed God because they hearkened to another voice instead of hearkening to God who had already spoken.

This means that, as a leader, you have to know the Word of God without question! You can't really function in full authority if you keep going back to the people and saying, "I'm sorry. I messed up. I'm sorry. I was wrong. I didn't really know." Does this put pressure on you to be right? Yes, you have to know in your spirit that you have heard from God.

ESTHER'S AUTHORITY

Esther functioned in full authority, but she didn't get there overnight. She had to go through a long process. The authority she ultimately exercised had to be developed. God did different things in her life in order to make this happen.

Lets examine this process by looking at Esther 2:8 (NKJV): *"So it was, when the king's command and decree were heard, and when many young women were gathered at Shushan the citadel, under the custody of Hegai, that Esther also was taken to the king's palace, into the care of Hegai the custodian of the women."*

The first thing that we see happening here is that Esther, a Jewess, is being shifted to another position. At first she was an unrecognized Jewess who was within the provinces of Persia, and then she is shifted to another position. Her position is now within the king's palace. We can easily see that she is already being set up for a position of authority.

Esther went from a position of not being known and of little or no significance to the palace of the king. She was an ordinary woman of Jewish tradition and background who was being transplanted into the palace. By a change of location she was being prepared for authority. This is important, because, if you're not in the proper location, your authority will mean nothing.

For example, you can be the Governor of West Virginia, but if you are in Canada, you will have no real authority. So it's important to recognize that in order for Esther to be set up for a position of authority, her location had to be changed first.

This is important to remember when it comes to authority in the church. To be in authority you have to be in the right position and the right location! If you are the music director in a church, you have authority in the music department. However, you cannot go to the Sunday school staff and dictate how they will teach and conduct their classes, because you would be out of position and carry no authority in their department.

Many times we see people in a church who have expertise, knowledge, and capability in a given area, but so often they are seated in the pews and are not in the proper location that would enable their authority to function in the church. We've got to recognize that God wants to shift people around sometimes so He can put them in the position that is right for them.

Therefore, the first thing we see happening with Esther (in verse 8) is that when the opportunity opens up for the maidens to come in before the king, she gets to move from the house on the hill to the palace.

The next thing that happens to her after she moves into the palace is that her attitude and mental outlook begin to change. This is true whenever your position changes. Why? Because you don't enter the palace in any way you choose. You don't approach the king in whatever way you choose. There has to be preparation. There is a fragrance and an adorning that you must put on, as Esther did. In fact, there are so many things that go along with being in the palace, that it took her a year just to prepare to meet the king.

Many young men have come to me and said, "God has called me." Then they run ahead, thinking that all they need is the call. God's callings need a time of preparation until God actually sets the person apart for ministry. When one gets ahead of God, he or she is likely to fall along the way, thinking that God has failed them.

It was years after Samuel came and anointed David and declared that he would be king, that David actually began preparing for the office. He had to wait on God's perfect timing. God spent years developing David to have the proper attitudes and character so he would be able to serve Him and Israel as king.

David went from a shepherd boy to a captain in Saul's army, then to a vagabond who was running from Saul and leading a band of 600 misfits, some of whom became his mighty men, to becoming king in Hebron, where he served for seven years. During this seven-year period, the rest of Israel watched him and finally came to him in Hebron and asked him to be king of all Israel. Even during his years on the run, he would send gifts to the elders of different cities in an effort to build his influence, and he always remembered the people he would eventually lead.

As I look back on my life and ministry, I can easily see how God moved me into positions that would help to prepare me for my current office of bishop. First, I was an evangelist. Then I became a pastor, and then I was elected to the office of a sectional presbyter in our district.

God continued my development by placing me in the office of District Secretary-Treasurer. Then I went on to serve the bishop as his "armor bearer" for seven years until he retired due to health reasons. Upon his retirement, God placed me in the office of bishop.

Each position was a preparatory step for each next place of service. It is important to realize that the office of a pastor is that of a servant, the office of a minister is that of a servant, and the office of bishop is that of a servant. To realize this requires years of attitude development!

In the case of Esther, we see that she had to go through a year of preparation just to be shifted into the right position so that she would be able to move toward her destiny and place of authority.

Esther 2:9-10 (NKJV): *"Now the young woman pleased him, and she obtained his favor; so he readily gave beauty preparations to her, besides her allowance. Then seven choice maidservants were provided for her from the king's palace, and he moved her and her maidservants to the best place in the house of the women. Esther had not revealed her people or family, for Mordecai had charged her not to reveal it."*

Now certain things happened to her at this point. She was moved into the palace, then she started to realize what it means to be in a position of power. She had certain maidens assigned to her, and she went through the rites of purification, which included both perfumes and adornment. The Bible says that she got the best position among the women in the house.

All of these things happened to her, and it seemed as if she had moved into a celebrity status or some kind of stardom. The realization of the change must have been somewhat overwhelming to her, for she went from "coach class" to "first class" almost overnight.

There are times when God does this to His leaders. Joseph was changed from a prisoner to a leader in one instant. Gideon was threshing barley while hiding from the Philistines, and he was changed into a great warrior and deliverer. Similarly, Saul was searching for his father's donkey's when Samuel anointed him as the King of Israel.

You cannot walk in authority with a street mentality, and you cannot walk in authority with a "pew mentality." You cannot walk in authority with a "submission mentality" either unless it is submission to God the Father.

You have to walk in authority in a way that causes everyone to recognize you as a true authority, someone who is in a different position than they are, but you must do this without making folks feel they are less than you.

One of the things that has happened in some churches today is that folks have moved into authority and they strive to make sure everybody knows it. They stick out their chests so far that you can't get close enough to hug them or even shake their hands.

Far too often in America we are smitten by stardom and well-known personalities and, unfortunately, this attitude has permeated into our churches. This causes some church leaders to adopt the same kinds of attitudes that celebrities in the world exhibit. It's hard to keep position and authority in their proper perspectives, but we must do so if we are to function in the authority God imparts to us.

Every prospective leader has to change his or her mind-set from the mentality of a follower to the mentality of a leader. When you are shifted into a position of authority and your time comes to be a leader, you have to make sure that you don't trip and fall into the same traps that have ensnared others before you. Be careful not to criticize them, however, because pride goes before a fall, and you could be the next one to fall into the trap.

What will you do when you are elevated to a position of authority? Will you be like the player in the batter box who is criticizing the guy who is up to bat before you? Don't forget that you are next, so be careful about what you say.

We need men and women who are truly different to rise to positions of authority today. We need their different levels of expertise and insight. We need their authenticity in the church today.

When Samuel anointed David as king, it was because God needed someone better to do the job. God chose a man who would not make the same mistakes that Saul made.

We cannot survive in a position of leadership if all we have is a notion or a theory. We must become absolutely and unequivocally immersed in the Word of God. Thus fortified in the Scriptures, things will happen when we minister. You cannot walk or lead on what you have heard someone else say. You must experience God's leading first-hand.

The Bible tells us that Esther was very keen and she understood her position. At the same time she was humble enough to follow Mordecai's instructions. He had told her, "Don't let people know right away that you are a Jew."

Sometimes one will cancel out his or her ability to go further in leadership because they "spill too much of the beans," so to speak. There are times when God wants us to share our whole testimony and times when He says, "Don't share it." There are times when you can't reveal everything about who you are until God has established you in the place where you are meant to be, because some people will immediately discount your ability when they learn what you've gone through.

I remember one time when I was speaking for a pastor who I had held in high regard for many years. He was one of the most knowledgeable men in the field of demonology and deliverance I ever knew. He had built a worldwide reputation in this field, and he had a radio broadcast and had written several books.

God had brought him from being a radical Black Panther and drug pusher to a great preacher of the gospel. Then, on this particular Sunday morning, he stood before the congregation and proudly declared that he had just earned his G.E.D.

I was flabbergasted by his personal revelation. I could not have ever imagined that this man had not been well-educated. He had earned great respect and had developed authority in God through the years. He had become an obvious student of the Word and an authority on demonology. For years he had traveled and set thousands free in Christ, without anyone knowing that he had never finished high school.

THE POWER OF INFLUENCE

Part of authority is having what I call "the power of influence." You can't have the power of influence in ministry if you release too much about yourself too early, for if you do so, people will discount your ability to be influential. I would estimate that at least 50 percent of your ministry is reputation! You cannot get into the pulpit and preach if you have a bad reputation. You cannot minister to people if they do not believe you to be a man of God.

If you start to mingle with the people in your congregation too much, you become may become too transparent, too familiar, and too common to them. As a result, people may have less regard for your influence and authority in their lives. I've seen this happen. The minister opens his mouth to speak, "Thus saith the Lord...," and the people say, "Oh, that is just him; you don't have to take that seriously."

My wife, Karren, and I decided to take a seminar that was being taught on marriage. It looked like a great course, and I wasn't disappointed by it. I was able to glean a great deal of information from the program. The instructors were a husband-and-wife team who were not from our area.

They were very interesting speakers, and they shared many illustrations from their lives together. On the second day of the seminar they told us that the reason they knew that the principles they were sharing worked was because the husband had been unfaithful to his wife and had had an affair.

I could understand the forgiveness and work that must have been involved in the healing of their marriage, so we continued listening to their teaching. After a couple of additional sessions, however, he said, "What we haven't told you is that I had more than one affair. I betrayed our marriage a second time after I was forgiven by my wife."

At that point we had heard enough. During the supper break Karren and I slipped out. Whether right or wrong, I had lost my respect for this man when he shared about his second act of adultery. My impression at that point was that he was undisciplined, and I wondered what would keep him from another affair.

Authority is the power of influence! That's why Esther had to hide certain things about herself. In Esther 2:11, we read that Mordecai was concerned about her. The Bible says that he became concerned everyday with regard to her positioning. He knew that her position had been changed.

Make sure the right people are close to you when you are in a position of authority, for many people will want to influence you and be close to you. Having the wrong person close to you or confiding in such a person could destroy you. Likewise, the wrong advice and opinions can cancel the effects of what God wants to do with your life and what He wants to do through you.

In Esther 2:17, we see that Esther obtained a key appointment! She replaced the one who had been disobedient to the king's wishes. The crown was then placed on Esther's head, and her position was right next to the king. Now she represented authority, royalty, power, and influence.

Princess Diana of the United Kingdom had great influence throughout the world. She was next to the future king in position and authority. The extent of her influence was phenomenal, for her style of dress, the way she wore her hair, what she did, and what she participated in became standards for women everywhere.

This was true of Esther, as well, after she had received her promotion from the king. This was the beginning of her ability to walk in authority. She now had the power and authority to move into places where other women could not move.

God specifically elevates certain people to positions of authority even when they are among their peers. You have to be careful about this, especially with ministers, because I find that jealousy can rage even among ministers and leaders. People can be literally driven and motivated by the fact that you've got something they don't have or the influence that they want but don't have. We need to realize that God exalts one and brings down another.

There is absolutely no place for jealousy in ministry. It is God who gives increase and God who gives promotion. I am convinced that one of Joab's problems was his jealousy of his uncle David. He stepped forward to gain influence on the day when David promised to make a general out of the man who figured out how to take Jerusalem.

We must have people in the pulpit who know their Bible. We need people who are well-equipped for ministry. These leaders must be well-disciplined, well-trained, and well-prepared. Such leaders will have great influence in the lives of many people.

If one of the large, international ministry leaders decided to set up a church in one of our cities, most of the little churches in the community would likely empty out. Do you know why? Because that leader has the power of influence on his side. He walks in authority, and many people who go to a little church in their neighborhood would drive 30 or even 60 miles to attend his church.

Believe me, this is true! However, we have to realize that it's not the largeness of the calling that we should be looking at; it's the expertise that we should be looking for. If you become an excellent minister and an excellent leader, and if everybody under your leadership functions in the context of excellence, the success you are looking for will come. Remember, though, you can't leave it to chance! It has to be planted, cultivated, groomed, and developed. There is no room for complacency in leadership today.

Esther received a key appointment. She was properly located and positioned. Esther had to make sure that she got her promotion. She could not become complacent.

And the Bible tells us, *"The king loved Esther more than all the other women, and she obtained grace and favor in his sight more than all the virgins; so he set the royal crown upon her head and made her queen instead of Vashti"* (Esther 2:17 NKJV).

CHAPTER 17

NOT FORGETTING THOSE YOU SERVE

(DEFEAT COMPLACENCY)

ESTHER has left the villages of Persia. No longer does she have to go to the well in the morning for water and carry it back home on her head. She no longer has to mend and sew and cook the meals, and she doesn't have to go down to the riverbank to do the wash. Now she is in Shushan, the palace. She no longer has to worry about how her food will be cooked. She no longer worries about her perfume, because the fragrance she uses now has been specially designed for her. In fact, she doesn't worry about anything.

She simply gets up in the morning and goes to her bath which is prepared for her. She's catered to, she's pampered, she's touched, she's massaged, she's given oils that are worked into her body, her hair is groomed properly, and only the finest silks are laid out for her dressing pleasure. She is taken care of from top to bottom and no longer has to worry about anything.

Such comfortable and easy circumstances could cause Esther to become complacent. They could conceivably lead her to forget about her people who don't have the privilege of living like she does. Her new lifestyle could cause her to forget where she came from and what God has taken her out of.

In all of this we see a warning for everyone in leadership: Don't become complacent with your authoritative position, for if you become complacent, you may actually become too far removed from the needs of those you have been called to serve. When this happens, you won't know your audience, and your message will become irrelevant. You can lose sight of what is really important and what is needed.

This can easily happen when a leader has such a "good life" that he or she doesn't have to face any challenges anymore.

David knew his destiny and he kept in mind that God had made him king for the sake of the people, not for his own sake. Second Samuel 5:12 (NKJV) says, *"So David knew that the Lord had established him as king over Israel, and that He had exalted His kingdom for the sake of His people Israel."*

Later, in Second Samuel 8:15 (NKJV), we read, *"So David reigned over all Israel; and David administered judgment and justice to all his people."*

In King David, then, we find a great example for us to follow.

In spite of the luxury of her surroundings, Esther had to face a challenge that would test her call and attitude. We find this in Esther 4:13-14 (NKJV): *"Do not think in your heart that you will escape in the king's palace any more than all the other Jews. For if you remain completely silent at this time, relief and deliverance will arise for the Jews from another place, but you and your father's house will perish. Yet who knows whether you have come to the kingdom for such a time as this?"*

How important is Mordecai's warning here? After telling Esther about Hammon's decree, which he had convinced the king to sign, and after telling her that the Jews were about to be destroyed, he wanted her to know that just because she was in the king's house did not mean she would get away without being hurt or harmed.

There is something in this story for every leader to learn. This is a challenge that you may face as a leader, as well. When various circumstances and challenges come into the lives of those you lead, if you are too far removed from them, you might be tempted to think, "Oh, that's not going to touch us, its not going to affect us, not my family and my house."

Do you remember the attitude of Shammah—the man who would fight over someone else's pea patch? He was a man who would give of himself for others. Shammah was a man of perseverance, one you could count on to be there when you need him. This type of leader won't turn and run in the face of adversity.

When the challenges come, as a leader, you must be concerned about them even if they do not directly affect you and yours. One of the reasons why you are in authority is because your position will help others face their challenges.

The challenge comes and God gives you, as His leader, the vision to help you know how the challenge can be responded to most effectively. That's what every leader is called to do. Many times leaders are able to see what their followers may not or cannot see.

What qualifies a person to be an anointed leader can be seen in the contrast between David and Saul. One looked like a king; Saul was head and shoulders over the rest of Israel. David, on the other hand, knew how to pray and worship.

Earthly credentials are fine, but what we really need to check is a leader's spiritual credentials and his or her prayer life. Other important criteria relate to the person's moral life, social life, and relationships.

I once heard a Christian lawyer state that when she interviewed a prospective employee, she would ask the candidate what his or her favorite television show was. Then she would ask him or her to tell him what their best friend's occupation was. She explained that you can learn a great deal about a person by asking questions about their social life and how they spend their spare time. I'm sure she's exactly right about this.

In many ways this is a biblical approach. When you read the biblical Books of Timothy and Titus, in which Paul spells out the main qualifications for leadership within the Church of Jesus Christ, we see many important questions being raised: How many wives does the prospective leader have? How does he discipline his children? Does he drink? Is he greedy for power and money?

The leaders of the New Testament church were required to have a good reputation that was based on good behavior. The leader must not be a novice, because becoming a leader too early will often lead to pride which can easily bring a leader down.

Other questions that would be appropriate to ask a prospective leader might include the following: What do his or her neighbors say about him? How many hours does he or she spend in prayer each week? Are his or her children saved? What kind of neighbors does he or she have? (Many times our neighbors are directly influenced by us.)

True leadership is developed in the heart. In fact, it begins in the womb, because true leadership is ordained and mandated by God! We, the Church, must not be afraid of risks, and we must realize that some of the people God wants you to place in leadership may not necessarily fit into the typical "box."

Peter was a fisherman. Levi was a tax collector. John was a young man. These guys weren't prepared to lead the church when Jesus left. But what did He give them? He gave them the mark of authenticity, for they had been with Him, and they were anointed with the power of the Holy Spirit. Therefore, they were fully capable of leading His Church.

Like those disciples, Esther was being "prepped" to face the challenges that always come with a position of leadership. Through her life we see that there must be a response to every challenge, and challenges will certainly come your way. They help you see if you are really prepared to walk in authority. Your response to these challenges shows whether you are truly prepared for leadership.

Esther did not respond to the challenge by saying, "No, I live in the palace. My schedule is too full. My servants are caring for me right now, so I'll get back to you later."

She could not move away from the challenges and feel comfortable, for she now occupied a position of authority. She knew she had to respond in a way that might even put her life on the line, which is what we, as leaders, are called to do for the people we pastor.

David understood that leadership was service. Years before, as a shepherd boy, he had learned that a shepherd is responsible for his sheep. If a bear or lion were to threaten the flock, he knew he had to put his life on the line for the sheep.

This attitude is one of the major things that enable us to rise into positions of authority. Godly leadership must be willing to risk everything. People won't really be able to trust you until you put everything on the line for them. That's when leadership is really established.

Our authority is going to grow as a result of our trustworthiness. If you are to have unquestioned authority with a group or an individual you are ministering to, they have to trust you. This is a challenge in our present age because of certain indiscretions in leader's lives that people have heard about. Because of this, you must build a trusting relationship with your people.

Isaiah 12:2 says, *"Behold, God is my salvation, I will trust and not be afraid."* This statement of faith is the basis of trust in all our relationships. Trust can be earned, lost, violated, and it can be restored. It is the cornerstone of all lasting and effective relationships, and it is far more than a feeling or an emotion.

Indeed, trust may well be the single most important factor in building relationships, for it implies several things: accountability, predictability, reliability, and consistency. When you make a promise to someone, you make yourself accountable to that person. When a person knows that he or she may be called upon to explain his or her actions, that person has become accountable to others, and such accountability requires trust.

If God had said, "Hey, I'm God! I can do what I want, and you don't matter unless I decide that I want to show mercy to you from time to time. If I want to do so, I might change the rules tomorrow."

Such uncertainty and inconsistency would make it really hard to place your trust in Him. God, however, has made Himself predictable, reliable, and consistent in both His Word and our lives. In fact, God has told us that He will never change!

When trust is violated, it is difficult to restore. As believers, we must act on God's Word and forgive the indiscretions, hurts, failures and betrayals of another, but trusting that person is another matter altogether.

I have seen churches that have gone through a dozen pastors over a relatively short period of time. They have pictures of their former pastors on the wall. When a church has gone through ten pastors in twelve years, that church must have trust issues. There is also a good possibility that such a church deals with rebellion issues, as well. Proverbs 28:2 (NKJV) says, *"Because of the transgression of a land, many are its princes."*

Mordecai made it clear to Esther that she was replaceable. God could raise up somebody else, if she were to become too complacent or comfortable. If God has placed you in a leadership position, it's important for you to realize that He is depending on you to come through.

In chapter seven of the Book of Esther, we learn that authority requires wisdom which will ensure that your influence is used in the right way. We must remember the biblical truths that pride goes before a fall and a haughty spirit precedes destruction. (See Proverbs 16:18.)

Have you ever seen a person who moved into a position of authority and then everything about them, including attitudes and behaviors, seemed to change?

When Solomon first became king over Israel, God asked him, "Solomon, what is it that you want? You can ask for anything, and I will give it to you!"

Solomon said, "God, give me wisdom and understanding." This should be our prayer, as well, for, as leaders, we need all the wisdom and understanding we can get in order to be effective in exercising our authority.

Esther found herself in a position of authority. She was accountable to the people who did not live in the palace. Remember, she had kept her nationality a secret until this time. She has used wisdom.

Don't expect to be able to walk in the power to command, the power to influence, the power to judge, the power to determine, if you don't have wisdom.

In the Book of Esther 8 and 9 we see the king acknowledging her and her request. He gives the authority to write a royal decree to Esther and Mordecai. They could develop this document as they chose, and it would be in the king's name, sealed with his ring. The decree, therefore, would represent absolute, unquestionable authority, even though it was written by Esther. Once a document was sealed with the king's signet, it became irrevocable law.

Similarly, you and I represent the heavenly King, and when we speak forth His message and His Word, it is full of authority because His name is upon it. The Holy Spirit represents God's signet ring, and when you open your mouth as His representative, your words ought to be *"as the oracles of God,"* as Peter said. (See 1 Peter 4:11.) This is where you and I get our positioning in the eyes of the people. We are endorsed by the King.

> *"If anyone speaks, let him speak as the oracles of God. If anyone ministers, let him do it as with the ability which God supplies, that in all things God may be glorified through Jesus Christ, to whom belong the glory and the dominion forever and ever. Amen"* (1 Pet. 4:11 NKJV).

The position of authority which you and I occupy as leaders in the Church of Jesus Christ is similar to that of Esther and Mordecai, for we operate in the power and authority of our King, the Lord Jesus Christ. As we minister, people will recognize the King who has anointed us and endorsed and sealed our words.

It's very important to recognize that Esther and Mordecai were able to walk in authority only because they had gone through the necessary process of being raised up to a place where God could trust them with His authority.

As leaders, we must submit ourselves to God. When we do so, people will respect our position Likewise, we need to be closely knit together with authority, and we need to be familiar with authority. We need to be associated with authority. Before we can tell folks to follow our authority, we have to be personally under authority.

In Acts 4, when the disciples were asked by what name they were able to do what they did, their authority was being challenged. It's important to realize that authority doesn't come from a person's history, culture, group affiliations, organizational ties, or social connections. A leader's authority comes from the Name of Jesus and from the time the leader has spent with Him. It is interesting to note that the men who challenged Peter and the other disciples knew that these men had been with Jesus.

You can't walk in authority just because of you have a position or a title. The only authority that you will have as a leader will be established by the proof of God's anointing and by the amount of time you spend with Jesus.

SUMMARY

WHY were David's men such great warriors? One reason is that David taught them what he knew. In so doing, he reproduced in them what he was. David was a great warrior. He had been Israel's first giant killer. At Saul's request, he had slain 100 Philistines. He had fought bravely beside Eleazar and killed many.

He began his public career with what talents he possessed. He was a musician and a singer, whose talents had landed him a job in the palace of the King. Then, later, he used his ability with the slingshot to overcome one of Israel's fiercest enemies.

In his later encounters with King Saul, the king tried to kill him with a javelin as he played the harp. When he was on the run and living in caves, the opportunity presented itself for him to kill the king, but he respected the anointing that he knew Saul possessed.

David exhibited all the characteristics of those who later became his mighty men: bravery, loyalty, commitment, obedience, perseverance, prayer and worship, compassion and love, wisdom and discernment, and most of all, vision. He taught what he knew both by his example and his words.

In addition, some of his men were great warriors before they even met David. They joined him because he was a man like them. They could share his vision. He molded them by his own loyalty to them. He would stand with them in warfare. He did not stay behind and let them risk their lives alone. He was usually involved with them.

It's true that we attract people who have personalities that are similar to our own. These men were very similar to David in their attitudes and nature. So, we see that David's men had the very qualities of David himself. This was true even though they possessed different characteristics. Some were even greater warriors on the field of battle than David was, but some felt less secure than he did.

Joab, for example, was an insecure leader who was always looking over his shoulder to see if someone else wanted his job. David was sure to elevate men around him who could add strength to his weaknesses and make him stronger. He understood that someone might want his job, but no one could take his anointing. When God anoints you for ministry, that is yours and yours alone.

If you are a spiritual leader, realize that what God has given to you, no one can take from you. No one on this earth can take your anointing from you. Only you can surrender it through disobedience.

I remember one pastor who had eight other preachers who attended his church, and he desired to use them in ministry as much as possible so as to allow them to develop their ministries. He also knew they would be able to fill in for him when he was absent.

One time when he was in a meeting with these preachers, one of them asked him why he shared his pulpit so easily with them. He wanted to know if the pastor might be fearful that someone might take over and have him removed.

The pastor's response was similar to what I have just written. He said, "God called me to this place, God anointed me for this place, and until God is finished with me in this place, no one can steal my anointing."

David knew who he was: the anointed of the Lord. He knew he had been chosen by God to lead Israel, and he knew he had been anointed by the prophet for the job. Therefore, why should he fear other men? He knew they were exactly what he needed to become a great leader of Israel.

Why were these men so committed to David? It was because David led by example, and he knew that those who were closest to him would determine his level of success. He had the ability to recognize the abilities of others and how to use those abilities to help fulfill his purpose and vision.

David was a man who understood his position and that everything depended upon God. Giving the glory you receive back to God can be a hard thing to learn. If we don't do so, however, we will lose our strength in God. God must receive all the glory and the honor. When you read the Psalms, you can see that David understood this principle thoroughly.

There are times when we become distraught or fatigued and just don't feel like praising God. This is when we must give the "sacrifice of praise," as David did. (See Psalms 116:17.) We have to learn to get past the circumstances and enter into praise and worship.

There's a sense in which this truth can be applied to praise you receive from others as you minister. If someone comes up to you and shakes your hand and pats you on the back and says, "Pastor, that was really great; you really ministered to me" or offers similar words of praise, don't respond by saying, "I can't accept any praise; it was all God. He did it. I'm just an empty vessel." Such a response could well be insulting to the kindness of the person who is complimenting you.

Instead, accept what they say and thank them for it, but don't let the praise "go to your head." In a way, that is a sacrifice of praise, as well. We must offer it back to God at His altar.

The Psalmist asked, *"What shall I render to the Lord for all His benefits toward me?"* (Ps. 116:12 NKJV).

Many times insecure people who are like Joab never recognize their wrong attitudes. Instead, they will shift the blame or claim that their intentions were right. They will say that they were just misunderstood. Such people don't understand authority and proper team ethics.

We must keep in mind that God calls leaders, enables leaders, and makes leaders into servants, not rulers. You must never become complacent and develop the attitude that others are beneath you or that they are there to serve you.

Joab's example shows us how costly any form of disorder can be. Carnal natures and carnal perspectives always cause divisions. Paul teaches us that we should always be: *"Endeavoring to keep the unity of the Spirit in the bond of peace. There is one body and one Spirit, just as you are called in one hope of your calling"* (Eph. 4:3-4 NKJV).

No matter how gifted you are, it all comes back to order, structure, and Jesus. In First Corinthians 14:40 (NKJV), we read this important admonition, *"Let all things be done decently and in order."* If your life is not operating according to the laws of God, it is out of order.

Daniel didn't perform many great miracles, but his life was in order. If it had not been so, the lions would have eaten him. Because of one person's disorder, sin entered the world. Because of one serpent's disorder, all serpents must crawl in the dust. Because of Eve's disorder, husbands rule over their wives who must bear children in pain. There is always a price to disorder, as Joab found out.

Attitudes such as loyality, perseverance, respect for the needs of your leader, prayer, trust, commitment, discernment, and wisdom are what make great spiritual leaders. Such leaders are people of valor and acclaim.

Can attitudes be changed or developed? I believe the answer is yes. God's Word teaches us about the principle of putting off the old and putting on the new. Attitudes are developed by parents, teachers, reading, the environment, lifestyles and life experiences. All of these can be changed as we put off the old man and put on the new man, which is created by God. When we allow the Spirit of God to develop His fruit in our lives and natures, our attitudes profoundly change.

These fruit can be seen in the lives of godly leaders: *"But the fruit of the Spirit is love, joy, peace, longsuffering, kindness, goodness, faithfulness, gentleness, self-control. Against such there is no law"* (Gal. 5:22-23 NKJV).

The fruit of the Spirit form the attitudes of great leaders. They will enable you to become like one of David's mighty men.

DATE DUE
